Science Updates

最新科学の知見

Hiroto Nagata

Bill Benfield

photographs by
©iStockphoto.com

音声ファイルのダウンロード／ストリーミング

CD マーク表示がある箇所は、音声を弊社 HP より無料でダウンロード／ストリーミングすることができます。トップページのバナーをクリックし、書籍検索してください。書籍詳細ページに音声ダウンロードアイコンがございますのでそちらから自習用音声としてご活用ください。

https://www.seibido.co.jp

Science Updates

Copyright © 2016 by Hiroto Nagata, Bill Benfield

All rights reserved for Japan.
No part of this book may be reproduced in any form
without permission from Seibido Co., Ltd.

はじめに

　我々は自然の圧倒的な力の前に全くの無力である。2011年3月11日に発生した東日本大震災とそれに伴って起こった津波による壊滅的な状況に直面した我々は、そのことを嫌というほど認識させられた。また今世紀の初頭には人類に幸せを与えてくれると思われた科学技術、例えば原子力がひとたび暴走を始めると我々には止めようもないのだということが否定できない事実であることも明らかになった。このようにして我々は自然の猛威と科学技術の持つ悪い面が地球環境にもたらしてきた未曾有の破壊の跡を見てきたが、だからと言って自然を制御する努力や科学の暴走に枷を掛けるすべを手にする努力は未来永劫続けていかなければならない。そのためにも我々は科学の話題に目を向け生き生きとした関心を保ち続けることが大切である。

　本書はそのような現状を踏まえ、最新科学のさまざまなジャンルから24の話題を取り上げ、1. 予期せぬ出来事、2. 母なるどう猛な自然、3. 疑似科学を疑う、4. 生存戦略、5. 素晴らしき実験、6. 人体の不思議、7. 宇宙を探る、8. 未来へ向けて、の8つのパートに分け、平易な英語を使ってまとめたものである。理系だけではなく文化系の学生諸君にも興味を持って取り組んでもらえるものと確信している。

　本書を通して科学の楽しさが皆さんに伝えられ、そしてそれがさらなる英語と科学の学習へのきっかけになれば幸いである。

　最後になりましたが、本書の出版に当たりひとかたならぬご尽力を賜った株式会社成美堂の佐野英一郎社長をはじめ、編集担当の菅野英一、佐藤公雄両氏に、心より感謝申し上げる次第である。

2016年春

永田博人
Bill Benfield

本書の使い方

BASIC WORDS IN CONTEXT
　READING（本文）に出てくる単語の中でも特に重要な基本動詞を5つ厳選しました。全て学習英英辞典として評判の高いLLAD (Longman Advanced American Dictionary) で「語義定義用基本語彙」として使われている動詞を基に選んであります。

　演習は、下の欄から適切な動詞を選び、**必要に応じて形を変え**、（　　）内に入れて英文を完成するというものです。英文の内容は「生物環境」「自然資源」「医療」「生活様式」などを中心にまとめてありますので、基本語を使いながらこれらの話題を能動的に発信するための基礎固めをするつもりで取り組んでください。

READING
　450語前後の長さの科学的な読み物を集めてあります。「科学的」と言っても、専門的知識を必要とするようなものは一切ありません。日常生活で私たちが日頃目にし耳にする事柄を平易な英語でまとめてありますので、CDを利用するなどして本文を暗唱できるようになれば、最近メディアをにぎわせている科学的な話題を英語でつづれるということになります。ぜひ試して見てください。

COMPREHENSION QUESTIONS
　本文の内容を正確に理解したかどうかを確認するための質問です。CDを聞いてそれぞれの文が本文の内容と合致するかどうかを判断し、正しい場合には Tを、間違っている場合にはFを○で囲んで下さい。

USEFUL EXPRESSIONS
　本文中に出てくる熟語や慣用表現から、発信型コミュニケーションにも役に立つものを5つ選びました。日本語の意味を表わすように、英文の（　　　）内に下の欄から適切な語句を選び、**必要に応じて形を変えて**記入しましょう。

WRITING
　本文中に出てくる重要な構文表現を3つ集めました。日本語の意味を表わすように（　　　）内の語句を並べ替えてください。

SUMMARY
　本文を120語程度の長さに要約しました。本文の内容に合うように（　　　）内に適切な語を下の語群から選んで入れ、要約を完成させてください。

Contents

はじめに ... i

本書の使い方 ... iii

Part I Encountering the Unexpected （予期せぬ出来事）

Unit 1   Four-Legged Fish
進化の謎を探る ... 1

Unit 2   Reproduction Without Males
パパはいらない、ママだけで ... 5

Unit 3   Deeper and Deeper
深海の不思議な生き物 ... 9

Part II Nature, Our Ferocious Mother （母なるどう猛な自然）

Unit 4   An Explosive World Heritage
山体崩壊 ... 13

Unit 5   Fierce Fungi
深い森の地下抗争 ... 17

Unit 6   Extreme Weather
異常気象 ... 21

Part III Fact or Fiction? （疑似科学を疑う）

Unit 7   The Wolf Girls of Bengal
オオカミ少女はいなかった ... 25

Unit 8   Finding Nessie
ネッシーはどこだ? ... 29

Unit 9   Crop Circles
ミステリーサークル ... 33

Part IV Survival Strategies （生存戦略）

Unit 10   Smart Roots
気になる木の根冠 ... 37

Unit 11   Insecticide Resistance
耐性昆虫との闘い ... 41

Unit 12   Unwelcome Guests
寄生 ... 45

Part V   Wonderful Experiments（素晴らしき実験）

Unit 13   Galileo's Inclined Plane
斜塔には行かなかったガリレオ   49

Unit 14   All the Colors of the Rainbow
ニュートンとプリズム実験   53

Unit 15   Watching the Earth Move
フーコーの振り子   57

Part VI   Exploring Humans（人体の不思議）

Unit 16   The G Factor
知能とは何だ？   61

Unit 17   A Trip to the Land of Nod
眠りの不思議   65

Unit 18   Lab-Grown Organs
再生医療   69

Part VII   Exploring the Universe（宇宙を探る）

Unit 19   Looking for New Earths
新しい地球を探せ   73

Unit 20   Weird and Wonderful Worlds
月がとっても多いから   77

Unit 21   The Invisible Universe
見果てぬ宇宙   81

Part VIII   Toward Our Future（未来へ向けて）

Unit 22   Eating Bugs
虫喰う人々   85

Unit 23   Bacterial Batteries
シュワネラ菌で発電する   89

Unit 24   Carbon Capture and Storage
二酸化炭素回収・貯留   93

SUMMARY – 生物資源・環境関係名詞リスト   97

BASIC WORDS IN CONTEXT – 基本動詞リスト   98

USEFUL EXPRESSIONS & WRITING – 基本熟語・慣用表現・構文リスト   100

UNIT 1

Four-Legged Fish
進化の謎を探る

2004年、デボン紀後期の河川堆積岩の中から「ティクターリク」（大きな淡水魚）の化石が発見された。水生棲動物が陸上動物へと進化する過渡期の生物の化石はそれまで発見されておらず、「欠けた進化の環 (missing link)」と呼ばれていた。この発見に触発されたエミリー・スタンドンは、ティクターリクと同じように胸びれが四肢動物の腕のように発達し、えら呼吸と空気呼吸をするビチャーという現存の魚を使い、魚が陸上で生存できるかどうかの実験を行った。結果は驚くべきものだった。

▶ BASIC WORDS IN CONTEXT

1. We are now living in sterile boxes, (　　　　) sterile air and drinking sterile water.
2. (　　　　) trees along the main street gave our town a new look.
3. The old couple adopted an orphan and (　　　　) him with loving care.
4. It was a relief to hear that a thorough examination has (　　　　) that there were no real problems.
5. Ever since Billy (　　　　) some bad fish, he has avoided seafood like the plague.

| breathe | eat | plant | raise | show |

▶ READING   ① 02〜05

02 U.S. scientist Emily Standen was interested in the crucial evolutionary question of how fish traded fins for legs and developed the ability to walk on land. The discovery of Tiktaalik, a transitional fossil (more commonly known as a "missing link") of a fish with four limbs gave her an unusual idea. She decided to see if fish could survive on land. For her experiment she used bichir, a species that can breathe air and use their fins to pull themselves along on land

5

if necessary. The results were startling. The bichir became better at walking. They planted their fins closer to their bodies, lifted their heads higher and slipped less than fish raised in water. More significantly, their skeletons also changed. Their "shoulder" bones became longer and developed better contact with their fin bones. In addition, the bone attachments to the skull became weaker, allowing their heads to move more. And all these changes happened not over successive generations, but within the lifetimes of individual fish.

This phenomenon, known as plasticity, is not new in itself. We have known for a long time that our bodies can physically adapt to deal with many different tasks and environments. What Standen's experiment seems to show is that plasticity may play a part in evolution.

Evolutionary theory states that life evolves through genetic mutations, when a random change in a creature's genetic makeup gives it characteristics that enable it to succeed in a changing environment. Once this view became accepted, previous theories were dismissed. One such theory came from the 18th century French naturalist Jean-Baptiste Lamarck. He believed animals could adapt to changing conditions during their lifetime, and that these so-called acquired characteristics could be fixed in the animals' genes and passed on to subsequent generations. For example, it could be that giraffes have long necks because their ancestors were constantly stretching to eat leaves high on trees. Modern genetic theory, however, shows that an animal cannot pass on characteristics acquired during its lifetime to its offspring.

But Standen's results reinforce the belief of a growing number of biologists that animals may adapt first and mutate later, a reversal of conventional evolutionary thinking. It may be that plasticity can enable animals to "evolve" without evolving. In other words, permanent changes in their environment would lead to all members of a species developing the same way over generations. This means they would change without any alterations in their genes. The idea that adaptation can lead to actual genetic changes ruffles the feathers of most biologists, but there is no doubt that it presents a fascinating area for future research.

NOTES

bichir「ビチャー」アフリカ産のポリプテルス科に属する淡水魚。種類によって体長は約30センチほどのものから1メートル近くになるものまである。胸びれの付け根に筋肉が発達し四肢動物の腕のようになっているのと、浮き袋が2つに分かれ肺のようにガス交換を行いえら呼吸と並行して空気呼吸をするのが特徴。**Jean-Baptiste Lamarck**「ジャンバティスト・ラマルク」近世フランス王国のブルボン朝から復古王政にかけての19世紀の著名な博物学者であり、biology（生物学）という語を、現代の意味で初めて使った人物の一人である。彼の提唱した進化論は用不用説とも言われ、個体が後天的に獲得した形質は子孫に遺伝し、進化の推進力になると唱えるものであった。

COMPREHENSION QUESTIONS

1. [T / F] The terms "transitional fossil" and "missing link" refer to the same thing.
2. [T / F] Emily Standen experimented with Tiktaalik fish.
3. [T / F] Standen observed several significant changes in the fish she studied.
4. [T / F] Modern evolutionary theory accepts that animals can pass on acquired characteristics through their genes.
5. [T / F] Standen's results have changed what the majority of biologists believe.

USEFUL EXPRESSIONS

1. 木はくっつけ過ぎて植えてはいけない。間隔を空けてやらないとだめだ。
   Trees should not be planted too (   ) each other. They need to be spaced out.
2. 核兵器の拡散をこのまま放っておくと、人類は滅びてしまうかもしれない。
   If the proliferation of nuclear weapons is not properly (   ), the human race may be annihilated.
3. 研究者たちは、短期記憶において重要な役割を担う脳の2つの部位を確認した。
   The researchers identified two areas of the brain that (   ) short-term memory.
4. その企業は、再生医療に欠かせない技術の開発に成功した。
   The firm has (   ) developing an essential technology for regenerative medicine.
5. 臓器提供の必要性が世界的に増大しているが、そのために違法な臓器移植ツアーも増えてきている。
   The worldwide need for organ donations has (   ) a rise in illegal "transplant tourism."

| close to | deal with | lead to | play a part in | succeed in |

WRITING

1. 一度習慣をつけてしまえば、毎朝のジョギングもそう大変でもない。
   (becomes / once / it / habit / a), to go jogging every morning isn't that hard.
2. ほとんどの主婦は、いつもいつも物価が高いと愚痴をこぼしている。
   Most housewives (about / complaining / are / constantly) high commodity prices.
3. エイズは今や、私たちにとって最も重要な公衆衛生上の問題だということに疑いの余地はない。
   (doubt / is / no / there / that) AIDS is our most important public health problem now.

SUMMARY

 07

Biologist Emily Standen set up an (1.   ) to see if bichir fish could survive on land. She observed various changes in their bodies that helped them walk and hold their heads higher. These changes happened during the lifetime of the fish because of a (2.   ) known as (3.   ). Before current (4.   ) was accepted, some people suggested that animals could adapt to changing conditions and pass on these new behaviors to their (5.   ). Modern genetic theory states that this is impossible. Standen's experiment shows that animals may adapt first and mutate later, and that plasticity may enable animals to "evolve" without evolving. However, the idea that adaptation can lead to actual genetic changes is still disputed by most biologists.

| descendants   evolutionary theory   experiment   plasticity   phenomenon |

DID YOU KNOW?

ティクターリクは、フィラデルフィア自然科学アカデミーのニール・シュービンとテッド・ダエスクラーに率いられた研究班によって2004年にその化石が発見されたが、頭部は大きくワニのようであり、体長は3メートル近くにもなるような捕食獣だった。体はひれ、うろこ、単純なあごなどのような魚類の特徴と、頭蓋骨、首、強靭な胸部、上背部などのような陸上生物の特徴を備えており、さらに胸びれには手根関節があり、足のような働きをしていたと推測される。首の存在は、それまでの化石で初めて見られたものであった。

UNIT 2
Reproduction Without Males
パパはいらない、ママだけで

Parthenogenesis とは有性生殖する生物の雌が単独で子を作ることだ。生まれる子の性が雌のみならば産雌単為生殖（セイヨウタンポポ、増殖中のアブラムシやミジンコなど）、雄のみならば産雄単為生殖（ハチ、ハダニなど）、両性ならば両性単為生殖（休眠卵生産直前のアブラムシやミジンコなど）と呼ばれる。また、卵子が精子と受精することなく、新個体が発生することを単為発生という。

▶ BASIC WORDS IN CONTEXT

1. The idea that man would someday fly to the moon was once (　　　) to be so much nonsense.
2. I (　　　) a bad cold and had to take things easy at home for a couple of days.
3. These malarial parasites (　　　) asexually in the mammalian host's red blood cells.
4. After the flood, we (　　　) all day mopping up the water covering the floors.
5. Biologically humans and apes are very close, but that doesn't necessarily mean that human beings (　　　) from apes.

> catch　　evolve　　reproduce　　spend　　think

▶ READING

① 08〜13

08 What do some sharks, boa constrictors, turkeys and Komodo dragons have in common? The answer is parthenogenesis or virgin birth. In other words, some female members of these species have the ability to give birth without ever coming into contact with a male of the same species. For a time, it was thought that this phenomenon occurred only when the animals were in captivity, but

5

there is increasing evidence that it also happens in the wild.

09 Researchers recently analyzed the litters of pit vipers caught when they were already pregnant. Two of these litters were the result of virgin birth, but the female snakes were caught in an area where there were lots of males, which means that this kind of birth does not happen simply as a last resort when males are scarce.

10 In some ways, a female-only population makes sense. Because every member of the group can reproduce, the population will grow faster, and if they do not have to waste time looking for a mate, they can spend more time searching for food. However, research into female-only species seems to suggest that their survival is limited to between 10,000 and 100,000 generations. This is because without males, they are unable to reshuffle their genome to get rid of harmful mutations.

11 But there is one all-female species of fish, called Amazon mollies, that is 280,000 years, or 800,000 generations, old. There is another all-female species of mole salamander that lives around the Great Lakes region of North America. It is estimated that this species appeared around five million years ago, and so it has survived for about one million generations. These species have a secret to their long life: they steal DNA.

12 In the case of Amazon mollies, even though they reproduce by parthenogenesis, they initiate the reproductive process by mating with a male fish of a related species. The DNA from this male is then normally discarded, but it is occasionally incorporated into the genome of the offspring. This enables the animals to produce offspring that are better suited to their environment in the same way that sexual animals do. This means that unless all-female species can steal genetic material from males of another species, they will not survive long.

13 Species cannot slowly evolve into all-female species. The general pattern seems to be that unisexual species are created spontaneously by the interbreeding of two related species. This mixing of two genomes can create a kind of strength and resilience known as "hybrid vigor," which is a phenomenon observed when plants are crossbred. But despite the presence of these single-sex anomalies in nature, it seems that virgin birth in the animal kingdom is likely to be restricted to a very small number of species.

Unit 2 – *Reproduction Without Males*

NOTES

parthenogenesis「単為［処女］生殖」　**in captivity**「監禁状態(動物園で)」↔ in the wild　**litter**「(動物の)一腹の子」　**Amazon molly**「アマゾンモーリー」カダヤシ属の熱帯魚　**mole salamander**「マルクチサンショウウオ」　**hybrid vigor**「雑種強勢」雑種の子が親よりも丈夫さや成長の速さなどで勝っていること＝ heterosis。

COMPREHENSION QUESTIONS

1. [T / F] Parthenogenesis is much more common among animals in the wild than among those in captivity.
2. [T / F] Virgin birth does not necessarily occur when there is a shortage of males.
3. [T / F] Virgin birth will normally place a limit on the life span of a species.
4. [T / F] The DNA of males with whom Amazon mollies mate never appears in their offspring's genome.
5. [T / F] Unisexual species seem to be created by accident rather than by evolution.

USEFUL EXPRESSIONS

1. 妹のルースは昨夜、健康で元気な男の赤ちゃんを産んだ。
   My sister Ruth (　　　　) a healthy, bouncing baby boy last night.
2. 嵐が来るということなので、すぐに荷物をまとめてこのキャンプ場から退散した方がよい。
   Because of the coming storm, it (　　　　) to pack up and leave this camping site right away.
3. そのようなカビの生えたような古臭い考えを捨てなければ、君はこの研究分野では決して成功しないよ。
   You'll never get anywhere in this field of research if you don't (　　　　) those old stick-in-the-mud ideas.
4. 水はまだ濁っている。つまり、浄化装置を改善する必要があるということだ。
   The water is still cloudy; (　　　　), we need to improve our purification devices.
5. ひょうを伴った大嵐による我が家への被害は瓦数枚に限られていた。
   The damage to our house from the big hailstorm (　　　　) a few roof tiles.

> be limited [restricted] to　　give birth to　　get rid of
> in other words　　make sense

WRITING

1. 台風による被害は10億円を超えるだろうと見積もられている。
   (is / damage / that / it / caused / estimated / the) by the typhoon will exceed one billion yen.
2. ドナルドは、性能が他のガソリン車に比べて劣るという事実にもかかわらず、環境に優しい車を購入した。
   Donald has bought an environmentally friendly electric car (it / that / the / fact / despite / is) inferior in performance to other gas-fueled cars.
3. 最近では「降れば必ず土砂降り」のように思える。実際、今、バケツをひっくり返したような雨だ。
   Recently (when / seems / it / that / it / rains), it pours. Actually, it's bucketing down.

SUMMARY

Parthenogenesis or virgin birth occurs in some species in captivity and in the wild. Virgin birth occurred in pit vipers caught in an area where there were lots of males, so (1.   ) of males played no part. The (2.   ) of female-only species may be limited because without males, they are unable to get rid of harmful (3.   ). But one all-female species of fish, Amazon mollies, has a long life because it steals DNA from males. They can therefore produce (4.   ) better suited to their environment. Species cannot slowly evolve into all-female (5.   ). Unisexual species seem to be created spontaneously by the interbreeding of two related species. This mixing of two genomes can create a kind of strength and resilience known as "hybrid vigor."

| mutations | offspring | scarcity | species | survival |

DID YOU KNOW?

mole salamander は北米産のマルクチサンショウウオ科のサンショウウオの総称。日本ではその代表格の tiger salamander から「トラフサンショウウオ」と呼ばれている。大きなものでは体長30センチ、小さなものは十数センチで、一生のほとんどを水辺の地下で過ごす。かつて、ウーパールーパーと呼ばれたメキシコサラマンダー（Ambystoma mexicanum）も、この仲間。

UNIT 3

Deeper and Deeper

深海の不思議な生きもの

深海とは海面下 200 メートルより深い海を指すが、太陽光が届かない上に高水圧、低水温、低酸素などのために、生物は地上とは全く異なった環境での生活を余儀なくされる。特に高水圧に耐えるために、深海生物の全てに TMAO (trimethylamine oxide ＝トリメチルアミンオキシド) という化学物質が存在し、タンパク質が高圧下で分解するのを妨げているというのは、進化の奇跡と言えるのかもしれない。

BASIC WORDS IN CONTEXT

1. The dentist told me that if he doesn't extract the nerve, my decayed tooth can't be (　　　　　).
2. Cockroaches (　　　　　) like mad during the hot and sticky Japanese summer.
3. Though he hadn't (　　　　　) a bike in years, it all came back to him soon after he cycled along the winding country road.
4. The original Kinkakuji temple no longer (　　　　　), as it was burned down in an arson attack in 1950.
5. Even after three years of severe drought, many farmers were (　　　　　) to stay and fight to the end to save their farms.

determine   exist   multiply   repair   ride

READING

① 16〜19

In the 1980s, the U.S. Department of Energy wanted to dispose of radioactive waste by burying it deep underground, but they had one major concern: below the surface, there might be microbes that could eat through the seals on the containers. Most people thought this unlikely because the deep earth was considered a sterile place where nothing could live. But to their great surprise, scientists discovered bacteria and single-celled organisms living 500 meters down.

Further discoveries followed, showing that life beneath the surface of the earth is in fact abundant, but it does not follow the same biological rules as life above the surface. These organisms are able to survive in an environment that lacks two ingredients considered vital for life — oxygen and sunlight — and where the supply of nutrients is very meager. When found and analyzed, some cells from deep within the earth seemed as dead as a doornail. A Japanese researcher, however, was able to determine that they were actually alive but had an extremely slow metabolism. This enabled them to ration a very small food source for thousands of years. Other organisms, discovered beneath the Pacific Ocean, used their tiny supply of nutrients to repair themselves rather than divide and multiply, which cells would do in normal circumstances. As a result, the same cells have survived in sediments deposited 86 million years ago, meaning they could be the oldest life form on earth. Microbes found in a South African gold mine are able to feed using hydrogen that is created when uranium decays and splits water molecules.

For a long time, it seemed that life deep below the earth's surface was limited to simple, single-celled life forms such as bacteria or amoeba. But in 2011, a team of researchers in South Africa found nematode worms — animals, and therefore a far more complex life form — at a depth of 1.3 kilometers, and then again at a depth of 3.6 kilometers. The researchers concluded that they probably rode down in groundwater that trickled into the earth about 12,000 years ago. These worms are able to survive because the water they live in still contains oxygen.

The discovery of life at such depths has forced scientists to change the way they think about life. These organisms, which can exist without oxygen or sunlight, may be able to provide clues about how life developed before photosynthesis began to make surface life abundant. What is more, the new insights we have gained from studying them may even help us in our search for life on other planets. Rather than examine the surface, it may be more effective to look underground.

NOTES

metabolism「新陳代謝」 **ration**「〜を一定量に制限する」 **sediments**「堆積物」特に砂などの粒子が風や水によって運搬され積もったものを指す。 **nematode worms** (= nema / round worm)「線虫」環節のない細長い筒状の虫の総称

COMPREHENSION QUESTIONS

1. [T / F] During the 1990s, scientists discovered bacteria living 500 meters below the surface.
2. [T / F] A Japanese researcher found some organisms that could survive without eating.
3. [T / F] The only kind of life forms found deep in the earth are single-celled organisms.
4. [T / F] Because of discoveries of life deep in the earth, scientists now have different ideas about life.
5. [T / F] Our search for life on other planets may be affected by our discoveries of life deep underground.

USEFUL EXPRESSIONS

1. ジャッキーが大変驚いたことには、その月の終わりまでには彼女は全部で5キロ減量していたのだ。
   Much (　　　　　), Jackie had lost a total of five kilograms in weight by the end of the month.
2. 浄水の研究をしている科学者たちは、このプロセスは他の浄化プロセスに比べ費用がかからないと主張している。
   Scientists working on water purification claim that this process is inexpensive when (　　　　　) other cleanup processes.
3. サイクリングの楽しさは、顔に当る風、髪を通り抜けていく風を感じながら坂を下ることにある。
   The joy of cycling lies in (　　　　　) a hill with the wind blowing in your face and through your hair.
4. ハチは人や動物が食べる食用穀物の多くの受粉に極めて重要である。
   Bees (　　　　　) the pollination of many food crops consumed by humans and animals.
5. 公害病で苦しんでいる人々のことを考えるとき、次は私たちではないかという奇妙な感覚にとらわれる。
   When I (　　　　　) people suffering from pollution-related diseases, I have a strange feeling that we might be next.

> be vital for　compared to　ride down　think about　to one's surprise

WRITING

1. 従って我々は、空気中と水中の二酸化炭素を正確に分析できるセンサーが必要となるのである。
   (we / sensor / is / need / therefore / a / which) capable of accurate analysis of CO_2 both in air and water.
2. 北海道地方の猛烈な吹雪のために、当社は今日からほとんどのフライトをキャンセルせざるを得なくなった。
   A severe snowstorm in the Hokkaido area has (us / forced / to / most / cancel / of) our flights starting today.
3. この情報は、自然と光合成のプロセスを理解するための手がかりを与えてくれるでしょう。
   This information may (clues / provide / to / nature / understanding / the) and the process of photosynthesis.

SUMMARY

① 21

We have recently discovered abundant life deep underground, which obeys different biological rules. It can exist without water and sunlight and with only a very limited supply of (1.   ). Some cells used their nutrients only to repair themselves and so did not divide like other (2.   ). Underground life forms are not only single-celled (3.   ), as we used to believe. Nematode worms were discovered in a (4.   ), living at a depth of 3.6 kilometers. Discovery of life deep underground has made scientists change the way they think about life. The (5.   ) we have gained from studying such life may help us in our search for life on other planets.

| cells   gold mine   insights   nutrients   organisms |

DID YOU KNOW?

太陽光が届かず高水圧、低水温、低酸素の深海では、全てが浅海の表層から降りてくる有機物のみに依存する世界だと思われていたが、1970年代から各国で進められた深海探査によって、そうではないことが明らかになった。例えば、海嶺や海底火山の熱水噴出孔の周囲では硫化水素などを摂取して生存する化学合成細菌や古細菌が存在し、さらにチューブワームやシロウリガイ、イソギンチャク、ユノハナガイなどの生物がいることが確認されている。

UNIT 4 An Explosive World Heritage

山体崩壊

山体崩壊は火山活動・風化・地震動などにより引き起こされる。山体崩壊が起こると山そのものが大きく破壊され、それが一気に流れ落ちる岩屑なだれ (debris avalanche) が発生する。山体の中でも細かく崩壊しなかったものは麓で流れ山という多数の小さな丘を作る。山体崩壊は噴火と比べると稀な現象であり、火山の一生の末期に起こるとされているが、例えば富士山の御殿場岩なだれなどのように、一つの火山で複数回発生することもある。

BASIC WORDS IN CONTEXT

1. Synthetic fiber is (   ) from materials such as gasoline and coal.
2. I (   ) clearly at the outset that I did not like the plan to resume operations at the nuclear facilities.
3. Modern medicine is learning that many traditional cures actually work, even though they were once (   ) old wives' tales.
4. Many victims of the earthquake were (   ) alive under the rubble of collapsed buildings.
5. Everybody is (   ) by the weather, not least the farmers.

| affect   bury   consider   produce   state |

READING

① 22〜26

The adoption of Mt. Fuji as a World Heritage site in 2012 reinforced the volcano's status as a symbol of Japan's natural beauty and religious tradition. But we should never forget that it is an active volcano, and as such, it can erupt with potentially disastrous consequences. The last time it did so was in December 1707. The so-called Hoei Eruption did not produce any lava flow, but scattered a thick cloud of volcanic ash that wreaked havoc in Osaka and spread as far as Edo, nearly 100 kilometers away.

23 Experts are now predicting that Mt. Fuji may soon erupt again. Some have even claimed that an eruption is "imminent." The Great East Japan Earthquake and its aftershocks that struck Japan in March 2011 may have put pressure on the volcano's underground magma chamber. A report stated that pressure in Fuji's magma chamber was measured at 1.6 megapascals. This is said to be much greater than the pressure just before the 1707 eruption and 16 times the 0.1 megapascal level considered necessary for an eruption to occur. In addition, there have been other warning signs, including steam and gas emitting from the crater, and hot natural gas and water being released from nearby massive holes. Making matters worse, the mud and landslides have created "temporary dams" in the mountain streams and rivers, which cause intermittent but incessant floods. Even more worryingly, they say that there is a 34-kilometer-long fault beneath Fuji. Some claim that if an earthquake were to occur along the fault line, the eruption could cause Mt Fuji to collapse, sending mud and landslides cascading down along with the lava.

24 Such collapses have occurred in Japan before. In 1792, Mt. Unzen erupted. The ensuing mud and landslides went straight into the Ariake Sea and caused a series of huge tsunami, which destroyed parts of Kumamoto Prefecture on the opposite shore, causing over 15,000 casualties. And on July 15, 1888, a phreatic vapor eruption occurred at Mt. Bandai. The subsequent mud and landslides wiped out and buried five villages, causing 477 deaths. The mud and landslides also dammed up the Nagase River, producing four lakes.

25 Experts say that an eruption could affect huge numbers of people and cause damage in excess of US$30 billion. If the collapse occurs on the eastern side of the mountain, some 400,000 people living in Gotemba City and along and around the nearby rivers could be affected. A northeastern side collapse could affect some 380,000 people, and a southwestern collapse, 150,000.

26 Mt. Fuji is an active volcano and will therefore erupt at some point in the future, either soon or many years from now. It is reassuring to know that the Japanese government is preparing for such an event and planning evacuation drills for areas that are likely to be most affected.

NOTES

active volcano「活火山」休火山 (dormant volcano) や死火山 (extinct [dead] volcano) などの言葉はあるが、惑星の年齢は100年以上の単位で考えるべきであり、休火山といえども活火山であるという捉え方のほうが安全かもしれない。　**temporary dams**「天然ダム」　**evacuation drills**「避難訓練」

COMPREHENSION QUESTIONS

1. [T / F] Lava flow from the Hoei Eruption severely damaged Osaka.
2. [T / F] Some experts believe that Mt. Fuji will erupt again very soon.
3. [T / F] The current pressure in Mt. Fuji's magma chamber is almost as high as it was before the 1707 eruption.
4. [T / F] The eruptions of Mt. Unzen and Mt. Bandai both caused mud and landslides.
5. [T / F] If Mt. Fuji erupts, it will affect at most 400,000 people.

USEFUL EXPRESSIONS

1. 天然痘は世界中の勤勉な医師や看護婦のおかげで根絶された。
   Smallpox has (　　　　　　) thanks to hardworking doctors and nurses all over the world.
2. 私の知る限りでは，宇宙人は3人だけだった—それ以外の宇宙人がUFOから降りるのは見なかった。
   (　　　　　　) I know, there were only three aliens — I didn't see any others get off the UFO.
3. 他の治療法も併用されない限り、投薬を中止すると症状が再発する可能性が高い
   Symptoms (　　　　　　) return when we stop medication, unless other therapies are also used.
4. 偉大な文学作品に加えて、ドイツ人詩人のゲーテは評価の高い数本の自然科学の研究論文を著わしている。
   (　　　　　　) his great literary works, the German poet Goethe wrote several well-regarded scientific studies.
5. マリアは有能な研究者です。でありますから、貴研究所に貢献することに何の問題もないはずです。（推薦書に用いられる決まり文句）
   Maria is an able researcher. (　　　　　　) she should have no trouble in contributing to your institute.

as far as	as such	be likely to	be wiped out	in addition to

WRITING

1. 記録によると富士山が最後に噴火したのは1700年代の初めごろだった。
   According to the records, (Mt. Fuji / time / the / erupted / last) was in the early 1700s.
2. 黒猫は不幸を招くといわれている。特に自分が歩いている道を彼らが横切る時に、そうだという。
   Black cats (to / bad / bring / are / luck / said) especially when they walk across your path.
3. これまで生存した恐竜の中で最大のものはアフリカ象のおよそ20倍の大きさであったと考えられている。
   The biggest dinosaurs that ever lived are thought (as / times / to / have / big / twenty / about / been) as African elephants.

SUMMARY

Mt. Fuji last erupted in December 1707. Experts are now predicting it may soon erupt again. Warning signs include steam and gas emitting from the (1.   ), and hot natural gas and water being released from nearby massive holes. Some claim that if an earthquake occurs along the (2.   ) beneath Fuji, the mountain could collapse, resulting in huge mud and (3.   ). Such collapses have occurred in Japan before, when Mt. Unzen erupted in 1792, and when Mt. Bandai erupted in 1888. Mt. Fuji's (4.   ) could affect huge numbers of people and cause damage in excess of US$30 billion. If the (5.   ) occurs on the eastern side of the mountain, some 400,000 people living in Gotemba City and along and around the nearby rivers could be affected.

| collapse | crater | eruption | fault | landslides |

DID YOU KNOW?

山体崩壊は土石流や洪水を引き起こすとともに天然ダムを生み出すが、時として源流部に多量の土砂が堆積し大雨のたびに土砂が流出するような事態を招くこともある。安倍川の大谷崩れ、常願寺川の鳶山崩れなどがその例である。しかしその反面、堰き止めによりできた湖が観光名所となっている例も多い。磐梯山の五色湖、駒ケ岳の大沼、小沼、箱根の芦ノ湖などがある。

UNIT 5

Fierce Fungi
深い森の地下抗争

糸状の細胞からなるカビは、特にジメジメした梅雨の季節に増殖し腐敗して臭気を放つ。人によってはアレルギーなどの発因ともなるが、その一方で薬品や発酵食品の原料ともなり、我々の生活に重要な役割を果たすものが多い。抗生物質の元となる菌もあり、抗生物質の効かない薬剤耐性菌に対する次世代の薬の開発にも期待が持たれている。

BASIC WORDS IN CONTEXT

1. Everyone (   ) to be playing ostrich while the world is threatened with nuclear disaster.
2. Our older son is feeling jealous of his new baby brother, probably because he feels his parents have been (   ) from him.
3. Somebody was (   ) by a bear not long ago, and the whole town was in an uproar.
4. A landslide (   ) the road, and we were stranded for several days in a mountain village.
5. I used to smoke like a chimney until my doctor (   ) me quit.

> attack   block   make   seem   steal

READING

① 29〜32

Biologically speaking, fungi have their own separate classification, being neither animals nor plants. But because they are commonly found growing in the ground, our first thought is to regard them as being more similar to plants than to animals. Genetic studies, however, have actually found that the opposite is true.

5

30 Fungi also seem to resemble animals not just genetically but also behaviorally, specifically in the aggressive tactics they use to acquire and defend their territory. Beneath the ground, fungi put out a mass of interlocking filaments called hyphae, which together form a mass known as the mycelium. As the fungi expand and move around in search of nutrients, these structures form the boundary of their territory. If two species of fungi encounter each other, a kind of full-scale war breaks out. One type of fungus can use its hyphae to coil around those of a victim and use enzymes to suck out food. Other fungi use chemicals or poison to kill their rivals and steal their nutrients. Fungi have also been found to use bullying tactics. If they have a choice of several opponents, they will attack the weakest ones first.

31 Fungi will not only attack other fungi but sometimes will also attack animals. Some fungi prey on minute worm-like organisms called nematodes. Using adhesive protrusions or hook-like growths, they can latch onto these worms and suck out their body contents. Even insects can fall victim to aggressive fungi. Normally, their hard outer shell can protect their interiors. But some fungi have the ability to penetrate these defenses and kill the insects by blocking their breathing tubes or spreading poisons.

32 These examples make fungi sound very scary, but scientists believe that it is possible to harness the abilities of fungi for practical purposes. For example, our best-known antibiotic, penicillin, is effective because of the tendency of fungi to kill microbes. And in the late 19th century, attempts were made in Russia and the United States to use fungi to produce insecticides. These attempts met with failure because of practical difficulties such as storage and distribution. However, with concerns about chemical insecticides growing, there has recently been a reawakening of interest in using fungi's natural chemicals to target specific pests. The one big problem so far has been that of getting fungi to produce the required chemicals in a laboratory setting. It seems that fungi can only produce their killer chemicals in the heat of an actual fight. If science can solve the question of what triggers this, we may be able to take advantage of their lethal talents to make better drugs.

NOTES

hyphae hypha（菌糸）の複数形　**mycelium**「菌糸体」菌糸の集まり　**bullying**「いじめ」
hard outer shell「外骨格」exoskeleton とも言われる。

COMPREHENSION QUESTIONS

1. [T / F] Even though fungi sometimes behave like animals, they are actually plants.
2. [T / F] Fungi develop underground boundaries to their territory.
3. [T / F] Fungi will attack both other fungi and animals in order to get food.
4. [T / F] We have not yet managed to successfully make medicine from fungi.
5. [T / F] It is difficult to make fungi produce their killer chemicals under controlled conditions.

USEFUL EXPRESSIONS

1. ジョーンズ博士は、人生の大半をアマゾンのジャングルで珍しい昆虫探しに費やした。
   Dr. Jones spent most of his time in the Amazon jungle (　　　　　) rare insects.
2. ワシは、ラットやウサギ、リス、イタチなどの小動物を餌食にする。
   Eagles (　　　　　) small animals such as rats, rabbits, squirrels and ferrets.
3. 野ウサギは、高い木の上で待ち伏せしていたジャガーの餌食になってしまった。
   A jackrabbit (　　　　　) a jaguar lying in wait for it in a high tree.
4. そのイオンは蛍光灯の光の中に見られるものに似ている。
   The ions (　　　　　) those found in fluorescent light.
5. 一行は冬山で遭難したが、飢えと寒さに耐え抜き、ついには救助された。
   The party (　　　　　) disaster in the winter mountains. They endured hunger and cold but were finally rescued.

be similar to　　fall victim to　　in search of　　meet with　　prey on

WRITING

1. もう今は腕をこまねいて見ている場合ではない。人口爆発の時限装置は刻々と時を刻んでいる。
   This is no time to just (arms / with / sit / your / back / folded). The population time bomb is ticking away.
2. マイクは以前はどうしてもすしを食べようとしなかったが、典子がようやく口にさせたところ、一度で味を覚えてしまった。
   Mike used to absolutely refuse to eat sushi, but he acquired an instant taste for it when Noriko finally (him / to / got / it / try).
3. 夫も私も音楽の才はないのだけれど、息子2人は初めから好きで自然に上達しているようだ。
   Though (nor / husband / neither / my / I) have an ear for music, our two sons seem to take to it.

SUMMARY

Fungi appear more similar to plants, but their (1.) seems to resemble that of animals. They use aggressive (2.) to acquire and defend territory. They can suck out food from other fungi or use chemicals or (3.) to kill them. They sometimes attack animals such as worms or insects. Scientists believe we can use fungi for practical purposes such as drugs. Penicillin, for instance, uses the ability of fungi to kill (4.). Previous attempts failed because of difficulties with (5.) and distribution. Another problem is that fungi seem to produce their killer chemicals only when involved in an actual fight. It has proved very difficult to make the fungi produce them in a laboratory setting.

| behavior | microbes | poison | storage | tactics |

DID YOU KNOW?

様々な食品に使われているカビの中でもアオカビは「ロックフォール」「ゴルゴンゾーラ」「カマンベール」「ブリー」などのチーズの育成に使われている。日本古来の発酵食品のみそ、しょうゆ、日本酒、焼酎などはニホンコウジカビを穀物で培養し繁殖させた麹(こうじ)を使って醸造されているが、納豆を作る納豆菌はカビではなく細菌の一種である。

UNIT 6

Extreme Weather

異常気象

気象庁では異常気象を「過去30年の気候に対して著しい偏りを示した天候」と定義し、世界気象機関では「平均気温や降水量が平年より著しく偏り、その偏差が25年以上に1回しか起こらない程度の大きさの現象」としている。そうなると、異常気象の原因としてよく例に挙げられる「エルニーニョ現象」は、数年に1度の周期で起こるものなので、異常気象ではないということになるが。

BASIC WORDS IN CONTEXT

1. When we began the journey along the African coast, little did we know the dangers we would be (　　　　　).
2. Environmentalists say the weather is (　　　　　) year by year, but is global warming a real danger, or are they merely crying wolf?
3. As far as I'm (　　　　　), either coffee or tea will do.
4. Criticism has (　　　　　) in reaction to the government's lack of disaster awareness.
5. Now that autumn is ending, leaves have (　　　　　) to fall off the deciduous trees.

> begin　　concern　　face　　rise　　warm

READING

① 35〜39

35 In July, 2013, devastating floods — called a once-in-a-century event — hit the Indian state of Uttarakhand. In the same year, Japan, Korea and China suffered extreme heat waves, which killed many people. In 2014, New Zealand had its worst drought for 70 years. In the same year, Europe faced heavy snowfall, storms and floods, and the Philippines suffered severe damage and loss of life as a result of the super typhoon Ruby. In recent years, such extreme weather events have become more frequent and more deadly. Not only does this extreme weather lead to loss of life and injury, it also destroys houses, factories and agricultural land, damaging crops and bringing severe food shortages.

5 　**36**　Many scientists are of the opinion that climate change is triggering this extreme weather. Climate change deniers, on the other hand, point to the recent spells of extreme cold weather, especially in the United States, to prove that Earth is not getting warmer. The majority of climate scientists, however, explain that weather and climate are not the same thing: weather
10 is what happens in the atmosphere from day to day, whereas climate is how the atmosphere behaves over long periods of time. As far as normal weather patterns are concerned, climate change has set the cat among the pigeons, and is likely to lead to many different kinds of phenomena.

　37　Average global temperatures are rising, but one area has begun to warm
15 twice as fast as any other area on Earth. This is the Arctic, where the ice-covered area is getting smaller every year. Experts now predict that the Arctic Ocean will be free of ice in summer by the end of the 21st century. The ice played an important role in reflecting back the heat of the sun. Once it has disappeared, it leaves behind dark ocean water, which absorbs more heat, and this results
20 in the ocean becoming warmer. This phenomenon may be connected to the increase in some of the extreme weather events mentioned above.

　38　The jet stream is a belt of fast-flowing westerly winds in the northern hemisphere. These winds effectively form a boundary between cold northern air and warm southern air. The jet stream is driven by the temperature difference
25 between the northerly latitudes and the tropical ones. Some scientists believe that as this temperature difference gets smaller, the jet stream will weaken. This has at least two major effects. Firstly, it means that it is easier for cold polar air to move southward, causing, for example, the extremely cold winters recently experienced in the United States. Secondly, as it slows down, weather
30 systems can get stuck in the same place for longer, leading, for example, to long periods of extreme heat.

　39　Because the loss of Arctic sea ice is a relatively recent occurrence, scientists do not have enough data to draw strong conclusions. But a strong consensus is emerging that climate change is having a powerful and dangerous effect on
35 Earth's weather.

NOTES

set the cat among the pigeons「（発言・行動などにより秘密などがばれて）面倒や騒ぎを引き起こす」put the cat among the canaries とも言う。 **the jet stream**「ジェット気流」大気中の圏界面付近の幅の狭い領域を流れる強い気流　**latitudes**「（ふつう複数形で、緯度から見た）地方, 地帯」

COMPREHENSION QUESTIONS

1. [T / F] In 2014, New Zealand suffered from a severe lack of water.
2. [T / F] Spells of extreme cold weather do not disprove that the global climate is changing.
3. [T / F] The ocean at the South Pole may be free of ice by the end of the 21st century.
4. [T / F] The jet stream blows from north to south.
5. [T / F] The slowing of the jet stream leads to weather systems staying in one position.

USEFUL EXPRESSIONS

1. 1970年代の後半までには日本の音楽界は変化し続けており、フォークソングや愛と平和の歌は時代遅れなものとなりつつあった。
   (　　　　　　) the 1970s, the music scene in Japan was changing, and folk music and songs about love and peace were becoming outdated.
2. 親の中には「プレッシャーのない教育」つまり「ゆとり教育」で学力が低下するのではないかと心配している者もいる。
   Some parents are worried that "education (　　　　　　) pressure," i.e., "education with latitude," might lower the scholastic level of students.
3. 自分たちの日常生活を改善するのには、その土地の人たちが積極的な役割を果たすことが必要だ。
   It's imperative for local people to (　　　　　　) improving their daily lives.
4. その地域の土壌は度重なる洪水でひどく浸食されていた。
   Repeated flooding has (　　　　　　) severe degradation of the soil in that area.
5. 肌の状態はその人の精神状態と密接な関係があることが知られている。
   Skin conditions are known to (　　　　　　) a person's state of mind.

> be connected to　　free of　　by the end of
> play a role in　　result in

WRITING

1. 数字の計算関係の仕事ならジェフの方がいい、と僕は思うけど。
   (that / of / opinion / am / I / the) Geoff is the better man for the number-crunching job.
2. 悪い天気がこんなに長く続くのは憂鬱（ゆううつ）だ。
   It's depressing when we have such a (bad/ long / weather / of / spell), isn't it?
3. リオグランデ川は米国とメキシコの境界になっている。
   The Rio Grande (the / forms / between / boundary) the United States and Mexico.

SUMMARY

① 41

In recent years, we have seen a large number of extreme weather events, including floods, (1.   ) and heavy snow and rain. People have been killed and injured, and buildings and crops have been destroyed. The (2.   ) has begun to warm twice as quickly as other areas of the planet and its sea ice is disappearing. This means the ocean will absorb more heat. The jet stream is a belt of fast-flowing winds in the northern (3.   ). As the difference in (4.   ) between northern and tropical latitudes gets smaller, some scientists believe the (5.   ) will weaken. This can allow cold polar air to move southward, causing colder winters. It can also mean that weather systems can get stuck in the same place for longer.

| Arctic   droughts   hemisphere   jet stream   temperature |

DID YOU KNOW?

異常気象の原因となっているといわれる偏西風とは、南北緯30～60度付近の中緯度上空の西寄りの風のことで、熱帯地域の加熱と極地域の冷却の極循環の違いにより発生する。偏西風は高度とともに強くなり、対流圏界面付近で最大となる。冬季にはこれが対流圏界面付近で毎秒100メートルに達しジェット気流と呼ばれる。

UNIT 7
The Wolf Girls of Bengal
オオカミ少女はいなかった

オオカミに育てられたという少女がインドにいた。発見された時には人間らしいところは全くなく、四つんばいで生肉を食べ夜中にはほえ声を上げた。養育者の献身的な努力で多少の愛情関係を築くことはできたが、知能や言語能力はほとんど発達しなかったという。幼児期の愛情や教育がいかに大切かを示す例として教育関係者の間でまことしやかに語られているこの話には、実はおかしなところが山ほどある。

BASIC WORDS IN CONTEXT

1. Despite a diagnosis of stage three stomach cancer, his wife and his family (　　　　　) him through to full recovery.
2. If the fire had been (　　　　　) a little later, it might have turned into a terrible disaster.
3. The mother looked out the window, smiled and said to her children, "Don't let Jack Frost (　　　　　) your nose."
4. Brown-bagging has (　　　　　) very popular among young office workers.
5. The effect of the painkiller (　　　　　) off very quickly, and my backache returned.

| become | bite | discover | nurse | wear |

READING

① 42〜46

42 All over Rome, visitors can see images of two baby boys being nursed by a she-wolf. These are the twin brothers, Romulus (the founder of Rome) and Remus. According to an ancient story, the boys were abandoned and left to die but were discovered by a kindly she-wolf, which nurtured them. This story is a legend, but there are also stories of real-life feral children who have supposedly 5 lost contact with human society and grown up alongside wild animals. The best known concerns the so-called "wolf girls of Bengal."

43 Joseph Amrito Lal Singh ran an orphanage near Calcutta (modern-day Kolkata) in the Indian state of Bengal. He said that one day in 1920, a man brought two girls, aged about two and eight, to his orphanage. This man claimed he had found them in the forest, where they had been living with wolves. Singh took the girls in, naming them Amala and Kamala. From his descriptions, the girls seemed more wolf-like than human. They walked on all fours; they could not speak but howled like dogs; they would accept only raw food and bit and scratched those who tried to feed them; and they preferred darkness to daylight.

44 Singh said he found it hard to train the girls to behave like humans. But after Amala died in 1921, Kamala apparently became more approachable. She eventually learned to put up with the company of other people, wear clothes and walk upright, and even speak a few words. She died in 1929.

45 On closer inspection, however, Singh's story begins to look like a hoax. He gave three separate accounts of how the girls were found. Originally, he said a man left them at his orphanage. He then said local villagers had rescued them from wolves. Next, he described how he and a party of men had freed the girls by attacking the wolves in a jungle. He kept a journal recording the lives of the girls, but he did not start recording his observations until one year after they came to him, and no independent experts verified his observations. He claimed to have photographs of the girls, but they were actually taken in 1937, years after both girls had died. A French doctor, who closely examined the evidence and wrote a book about the case, concluded that Singh was trying to pull the wool over people's eyes.

46 It may be possible for young children to survive in the wild alongside animals, but the probability is very low. It may be more likely that the girls suffered from a disability such as autism, and so their parents simply abandoned them. One theory is that Singh, who was not rich, wanted to use the story of the girls to make money for his orphanage. But in the end, no one will ever know the whole truth about the wolf girls of Bengal.

Unit 7 – *The Wolf Girls of Bengal*

NOTES

Romulus and Remus「ロムルスとレムス」ローマ帝国を築いたとされる双子の兄弟。オオカミの乳で育ったといわれ、銅像も残っている。 **autism**「自閉症」スイスの精神科医 Blueler の造語

COMPREHENSION QUESTIONS

1. [T / F] The story of the wolf girls of Bengal is just a legend.
2. [T / F] The two girls behaved more like animals than like human beings.
3. [T / F] Eventually, both girls learned to walk and speak a few words.
4. [T / F] Singh gave more than one explanation of how the girls were found.
5. [T / F] It is possible that Singh thought the girls would be useful to him financially.

USEFUL EXPRESSIONS

1. 特に若者にファストフードが大人気で、至る所にその店がある。
   Fast food is very popular especially among young people and there are shops (   ) the place.
2. 子供の頃は勉強嫌いだったが、彼女は長じて世界でも有名な環境保護論者になった。
   Though she hated to study when a girl, she (   ) to be a world-famous ecologist.
3. パイナップルの木は、昆虫の死骸からも養分の一部を取り入れている。
   Pineapple plants (   ) part of their nutrients from the bodies of dead insects.
4. カミツキガメの産卵場所を探そうとして、その生態学者は高く厚く生い茂る草の間を四つんばいになってはって行った。
   In an attempt to find the sites where snapping turtles lay their eggs, the ecologist went down (   ) and crawled through the tall, thick grass.
5. そのホテルの多くの客は、勇敢な消防士たちによって燃え盛る灼熱地獄から救助された。
   A lot of the hotel guests were (   ) the burning inferno by courageous firefighters.

```
all over    grow up    on all fours    rescue ... from    take in
```

WRITING

1. 未開の部族がたとえ近代文明の恩恵を取り入れられたとしても、それまでの古い生活習慣を捨て去るのは容易ではない。

   Even though primitive tribes may adopt the benefits of modern civilization, (to / for / difficult / it / them / is) turn their backs on the old ways of doing things.

2. 自著「沈黙の春」で殺虫剤使用の危険性に関して初めて警鐘を鳴らしたのは他でもないレイチェル・カーソンだった。

   (it / was / first / Rachel Carson / who) warned of the danger of pesticide use in her book "Silent Spring."

3. 早朝にこの通りを歩いていると、ノーベル生理医学賞を受賞された中山博士に偶然出会った。

   (morning / along / street / walking / this / early / the / in), I ran into Dr. Nakayama, who had been awarded the Nobel Prize in Physiology or Medicine.

SUMMARY

Joseph Singh took two girls into his (1.   ). They had apparently been raised by wolves and behaved like animals. They walked on all fours, ate raw food and bit and scratched people. One girl died, and eventually, the other one learned to wear clothes, walk upright and speak a few words. Singh's story is hard to believe. He gave three different (2.   ) of how the girls were found. No experts verified his (3.   ) of them. A doctor concluded that Singh's story was a (4.   ). It is possible that the girls' parents abandoned them because they were suffering from a (5.   ) such as autism. Maybe Singh, who was poor, wanted to use their story to make money for his orphanage.

> disability   explanations   hoax   observations   orphanage

DID YOU KNOW?

アマラとカマラの話には20数枚の「証拠写真」が残されている。ジャングルから救われた直後から2年数か月後の間に撮られらものとされているが、夜行性のオオカミに育てられたはずの2人が日中野外で無防備に寝ていたり、木に登ったりもする。背景や着ている物も同じなら、人が追い付けない程速く走ったという写真は背景も同じようにブレていたり、というように全く信頼性がないのだ。

UNIT 8

Finding Nessie
ネッシーはどこだ？

スコットランドのネス湖にいるという未確認動物。Loch Ness Monster として世界中に知られている「ネッシー」は 20 世紀最大級のミステリーの1つだ。恐竜時代に栄えたプレシオザウルスの生き残りであるという話は我々のロマンをかきたてる話題でもあり、今でもその大型獣が本当に生きているのではないかと信じている人も少なくない。

BASIC WORDS IN CONTEXT

1. You'd better (　　　　　) it easy on this road. There are a lot of sharp curves.
2. In (　　　　　) to the parents their child's chances of recovery, the doctor weighed his words with great care.
3. The first person to (　　　　　) that Earth is round was laughed out of court.
4. A typhoon raged across the Tokai district, (　　　　　) a great deal of havoc.
5. The doctors (　　　　　) the patient back from the brink of death.

> bring　　cause　　explain　　suggest　　take

READING

① 49〜52

On April 14, 1933, Mrs. Aldie Mackay, the manager of a hotel in the highlands of Scotland, was driving past Loch Ness with her husband. She glanced out of the window of the car across the loch and saw something swimming in a circle in the calm waters. She later described it as black and wet with water rolling off it. Though legends of a strange creature living in the loch date back to the 6th century, this incident is considered to be the first modern sighting of the creature now known as the Loch Ness Monster, or Nessie.

After Mrs. Mackay's husband reported her sighting to the authorities, it stirred up huge public interest. More and more reports came flooding in from people claiming to have spotted the mysterious creature. Tourists flocked to Loch Ness in the hope of catching sight of Nessie and maybe even photographing it. In 1934, a doctor took a now famous photo of a creature with a long arched neck sticking out of the waters of the loch. Like many photos that followed, this one was found to be a fake.

Various theories have been proposed to explain the alleged sightings of Nessie. One is that the monster could be an aquatic dinosaur called a plesiosaur. This seems unlikely since plesiosaurs have been extinct for millions of years. More plausible explanations suggest that animals such as a seal, Greenland shark or eel could have somehow entered the loch, where they were mistaken for a monster. Other experts have put forward explanations based on natural movements in the water caused by phenomena such as ripples, boat wakes or escapes of gas from the bottom of the loch. More skeptical observers point to the large number of hoaxes, including faked video footage.

Loch Ness is not alone in having an inexplicable and elusive creature. Rumors abound of large ape-like creatures living in other parts of the world. North America has Bigfoot (or Sasquatch as it is also known) and the Himalayas have the yeti. People are certainly interested in catching sight of them, but the areas these strange beasts supposedly inhabit are enormous. Nessie, on the other hand, is confined to one loch, and so the likelihood of spotting it is much higher than running into Bigfoot or a yeti. As a result, Loch Ness swarms with monster hunters and curious tourists. It is estimated that Nessie-related tourism brings more than £1 million to the Loch Ness area every year. For the people living around the loch, especially those in businesses catering to tourists, Nessie is the goose that laid the golden egg. And the longer Nessie remains a mystery, the more profitable it will be.

Unit 8 – *Finding Nessie*

NOTES

Loch Ness「ネス湖」Lochはスコットランド・ゲール語で「湖」の意。英国最大の淡水湖。 **plesiosaur**「プレシオサウルス」首長竜の総称　**boat wakes**「航跡」船が通過した後に残る泡や波の筋

COMPREHENSION QUESTIONS

1. [T / F] The first modern sighting of Nessie was when a doctor saw it in 1934.
2. [T / F] One explanation is that Nessie is a very ancient creature.
3. [T / F] Some people think that natural movements in water may be mistaken for an animal.
4. [T / F] A creature called Bigfoot is supposed to live in the Himalayas.
5. [T / F] The story of Nessie results in good business for people in the Loch Ness area.

USEFUL EXPRESSIONS

1. 電気が初めて実際に使用されたのは、古代アラビア人の時代にさかのぼる。
   The first practical use of electricity (　　　　) the age of the ancient Arabs.
2. 園芸家は飛び出していた枝を切り落とし、盆栽を前より調和のとれた形にした。
   The horticulturalist cut off a branch that was (　　　　) and gave the bonsai tree a more harmonious shape.
3. 病気の原因は細菌だという考えを最初に提言したのは誰だっけ。パスツール、それともコッホ。
   I wonder who first (　　　　) the idea that germs cause disease? Was it Pasteur or was it Koch?
4. 私たちは実験手順を綿密に計画したが、ひどい落とし穴に陥った。
   We planned out the experiment procedures very carefully but (　　　　) a terrible pitfall.
5. その公園には、デング熱を媒介すると考えられていた蚊が群れをなして飛び回っていた。
   The park was (　　　　) mosquitoes that were believed to carry dengue fever.

> date back to　　put forward　　run into　　stick out　　swarm with

WRITING

1. その患者は完全に治るという希望を持って最後の闘病生活を送っていた。
   The patient spent his final days in the hospital (total / of / the / in / cure / a / hope).
2. 自らの論文の研究結果の不正書き換えに彼女自身が関わっていたといううわさが飛び交っている。
   (that / involved / she / abound / rumors / was) in doctoring the research results in her paper.
3. 雨が降ったりやんだりでさすがにうっとうしく感じるが、逆に今年は水不足はなさそうだ。
   It's been raining day in and day out and it's starting to get me down. (other / the / but / on / hand), it's unlikely that we'll have a water shortage this year.

SUMMARY

The first modern (1.   ) of the Loch Ness Monster took place in 1933, but (2.   ) of the creature go back to the 6th century. After (3.   ) became public, tourists flocked to the area to try to see Nessie or take a picture of it. Many photos of the monster turned out be (4.   ). One theory is that Nessie is a dinosaur. Another is that people may have seen animals such as a seal, shark or eel. Alternatively, people could have seen natural movements such as ripples in the water and mistaken them for a living creature. Nessie still attracts many tourists to Loch Ness, bringing a good (5.   ) to people who live in the area.

| fake   income   legends   reports   sighting |

DID YOU KNOW?

1934年4月にデイリー・メール紙に掲載されたネッシーの写真は「外科医の写真」として有名になったが、後に実はオモチャの潜水艦に恐竜の首を付けたものでエイプリール・フールのジョークのつもりだったという告白があった。首長竜は実際には陸生であったらしいことも分かり当時の熱気は一段落したが、最近でも数度にわたって大規模確認調査が行われるなど、まだまだその存在を信じたい人は多い。

UNIT 9

Crop Circles
ミステリーサークル

穀物が円形になぎ倒され複雑な形状を残す「ミステリーサークル」は英国を中心に世界中に出現している。1980年代謎の現象として注目されたこの現象には宇宙人説や超常現象説などさまざまな原因仮説があったが、1991年に英国のDoug BowerとDave Chorleyの2人が簡単な道具を使い、比較的短時間に作り出し、人為的ないたずらだったとみなされるようになった。だが、いたずらでは説明できないサークルも現に存在するようだ。

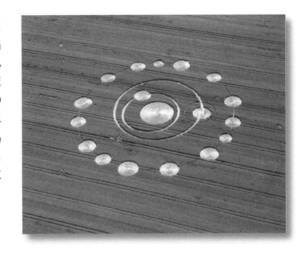

BASIC WORDS IN CONTEXT

1. The temperature dropped so much that ice has (   ) on the pond.
2. Following my near-death experience, the whole world (   ) to me in a different light.
3. The hospital is (   ) free health care to people who are willing to serve as guinea pigs for a new medicine.
4. I could have (   ) directly to Atlanta, but I decided to break my trip in San Francisco.
5. This tropical disease is so rare that only five cases have been (   ).

| appear | fly | form | offer | report |

READING

① 55〜60

One morning in the early 1980s, a farmer in a village in the west of England could not believe his eyes. During the night, someone — or something — had flattened part of the crops in his field to form three circles, each 18 meters across. There had been reports of similar occurrences since the 1960s, but this time, the media took an interest, and the public became aware of the phenomenon known as crop circles.

Since that time, crop circles have been appearing in fields in many different countries. The word "circles" is a bit misleading, however. The designs are often extremely elaborate. Some even represent sophisticated mathematical concepts like the value of pi or fractal equations. Naturally, they captured people's imagination. Several explanations were offered, ranging from the scientific to the supernatural. Some people believed extraterrestrials were responsible. They flattened the crops using rays of energy from hovering spaceships with the intention of delivering coded messages to humanity. Others thought that the patterns were created by a natural but mysterious energy in the earth.

In 1991, however, a simpler explanation seemed to emerge. Two British men told the media that they had been sneaking into fields in the middle of the night since 1978 and creating the patterns using boards, ropes and wooden barrels to flatten the crops. When people expressed disbelief, the two men actually demonstrated to watching reporters how they did it. The patterns they created were so similar to those that had already been found that the mystery appeared to be solved: crop circles were nothing but an elaborate prank.

But perhaps there is more to the story than meets the eye. In 1996, a pilot was flying a small plane near Stonehenge in the southwest of England. He passed over a field at 5:30 and saw nothing unusual. Passing over the same field again less than an hour later, he noticed a very complex pattern. (It has since been named the "Julia Set," after the complex mathematical fractal it represents.) Eyewitnesses on the ground reported seeing a cloud of mist hovering over the field, creating the pattern.

Crop circles have also pricked the curiosity of an archeology specialist at the University of Tasmania in Australia. He believes that not all crop circles are the work of humans, but his explanation is scientific rather than supernatural. After spending more than 300 hours analyzing photos from 1945 on Google Earth, he concluded that crop circles had been appearing in England for at least 33 years before the two hoaxers made their announcement. He believes the cause might be a rare form of electromagnetic energy called an ionized plasma vortex, or ball lightning.

Even though the majority of crop circles are probably made by people for fun or media attention, doubt remains that human beings are responsible for every single one.

Unit 9 – *Crop Circles*

NOTES

fractal「フラクタル」どんな細部を見ても全体と同じ構造が現れる多次元分裂図形。フランス人数学者ブノア・マンデルブロ (Benoît Mandelbrot) が紹介した概念。　**ball lightning**「球電光」発光体が空中を浮遊する現象。雷雨の際に多く見られ、赤から黄色の光を放つものが多い。直径10〜30センチぐらいの火球が数十秒間動き回って消失する。

COMPREHENSION QUESTIONS　① 61

1. [T / F]　The crop circle found in the 1980s was not the first one that was discovered.
2. [T / F]　The patterns consist of simple circles.
3. [T / F]　Some people believe that science cannot explain crop circles.
4. [T / F]　Two British men admitted that they had created the crop circles as a kind of joke.
5. [T / F]　A scientist from the University of Tasmania believes extraterrestrials create crop circles.

USEFUL EXPRESSIONS

1. 年を取れば取るほど，世代間の断絶をそれまで以上に意識するようになる。特に社会の高齢化がこれほど早く進むと、そうなる。
   The older you get, the more you (　　　　　) the generation gap, especially when society ages this fast.
2. 試料は35〜65歳の患者10人の膝関節から採取された。
   Samples were obtained from the knee joint in ten patients (　　　　　) in age (　　　　　) 35 (　　　　　) 65 years.
3. 真夏の真っ昼間に激しい運動をさせるなんて、熱中症患者を自ら作り出すようなものだ。
   Making people do strenuous exercise (　　　　　) the day in the summertime will inevitably produce heat-stroke patients.
4. ブラウン博士は自分の犬を、ポーランドのかの有名な天文学者にちなんでコペルニクスと名付けた。
   Dr. Brown (　　　　　) his dog Copernicus (　　　　　) the famous Polish astronomer.
5. その医師は私に、手術は成功したが、父が危機を脱するまでには少なくともあと48時間はかかるだろうと言った。
   The doctor told me that the operation was successful, but my father won't be out of danger for (　　　　　) another 48 hours.

> at least　　become aware of　　in the middle of
> name ... after　　range from ... to

WRITING

1. 夏休みは山で過ごす方が良いと言う人もいるが、海の方がいいと言う人もいる。
   (might / some / people / say / that) it's better to spend summer vacation in the mountains, (others / say / might / but) it's better at the beach.
2. 全ての発明家が自分の発明の功績を認められるわけではない。時として他の誰かが自分の手柄にしてしまうこともある。
   (not / for / all / credit / inventors / get) their discoveries. At times someone else takes it.
3. 世界中の石油埋蔵量が急速に減らされていったにもかかわらず、先進諸国はその不吉な前兆を無視し続けた。
   (oil / the / reserves / even / world's / though) were rapidly being depleted, the advanced nations continued to ignore the writing on the wall.

SUMMARY

Crop circles are designs, sometimes very elaborate, that are created in fields by flattening the crops growing there. Some people believed that they were created by (1.   ) as a way of giving messages to humanity. In 1978, two British men admitted that they had created the designs as a joke, using (2.   ) and ropes. But in 1996, a pilot flew over a field in the west of England and saw nothing unusual. One hour later, he flew over the same field again and noticed a very complex (3.   ). After studying old photographs, an (4.   ) specialist believes that crop circles appeared in England before the two men announced their hoax. He thinks electromagnetic (5.   ) may be responsible.

| archeology | boards | energy | extraterrestrials | pattern |

DID YOU KNOW?

今では人間によるいたずらだとして片付けられているミステリーサークルだが、それでは説明がつかないケースもあると主張する人たちがいる。ダウンバースト（下降噴流）やプラズマ（電離気体）に科学的原因を求める人もあるが、宇宙人からのメッセージだという思いが捨てられない人も多い。

10 UNIT

Smart Roots
気になる木の根冠

光合成をする植物が誕生したのはおよそ30億年前だった。昆布のように海中を漂っていたらしい。それが陸上で進化しキノコやツクシ、シダのように繁茂して今の化石燃料の元になったのが石炭紀で約3億6,000万年前から3億年前だという。現在のように花が咲き、実がなり、種子が出来るような植物が現れたのが2億年ぐらい前。恐竜が栄えた時代、ソテツやイチョウのような木が多くなったころらしい。

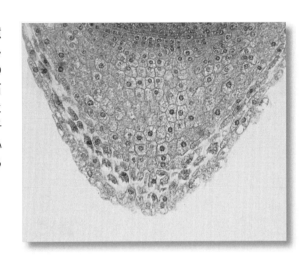

▶ BASIC WORDS IN CONTEXT

1. The WHO warned that China still (　　　　) the equipment and expertise to fight the disease.
2. We all should cut our intake of trans fats and (　　　　) foods.
3. Until recently, the operations of the brain were a (　　　　) book.
4. I was so exhausted that as soon as my head (　　　　) the pillow, I was out.
5. A camel (　　　　) a remarkable sense of direction and it can follow footprints.

close　　lack　　possess　　process　　touch

▶ READING

① 63〜66

What is necessary for an organism to be intelligent? The obvious answer is that the basic requirement is a brain. But is this necessarily true? Some scientists are starting to suggest that plants can be intelligent even though they lack a brain and the kind of nervous system found in animals. Scientists are beginning to discover that plants have a sophisticated awareness of their environment and of each other, and can even communicate what they sense.

64 The Greek philosopher Aristotle put human beings at the top of his "ladder of nature" while setting plants near the bottom, just above inanimate objects such as rocks. Charles Darwin, however, disagreed with this long-held view. He believed that a plant's root system acted like a brain. The root tip can sense properties such as gravity, oxygen, humidity, light and nutrients. Some scientists now believe that the root cap can transmit information to another part of the root system called the transition zone. This part processes the information and translates it into commands for the so-called elongation zone, which is responsible for controlling the growth and direction of the roots. Within the transition zone is a growth-regulating hormone that is carried around in protein containers, which behave in a very similar way to neurotransmitters in animal brains.

65 In addition, senses are extremely important to plants. In contrast to animals, which can move around to find food or escape danger, plants are rooted in one place. They therefore need the ability to sense their environment and act accordingly. It has been suggested that a plant's senses may even be keener than those of animals. For example, plants have photoreceptors that are extremely sensitive to both the quality and direction of light. Some plants also have what could be described as a kind of memory. The Venus flytrap, for instance, does not close its jaws on an insect when it is first touched. It will do so only if it feels a second touch within 30 seconds of the first one, exhibiting a form of "memory."

66 Scientific opinion regarding plant intelligence is divided. At one extreme, there are scientists who argue that plants can feel pain and may even be conscious. But the question of whether plants can be described as "intelligent" is difficult to answer, partly because there is very little agreement on what the definition of intelligence is, even in human beings. One eminent plant researcher has said that plants possess the various elements that make intelligence possible: sensing, awareness, information integration, memory and adaptive learning. It could be more accurate to say that plants do not possess intelligence but they undoubtedly have a high level of awareness.

Unit 10 – *Smart Roots*

NOTES

root cap「根冠」根の先端にあり生長点を覆う。ここに植物の脳とも言える細胞がある。
neurotransmitter「神経伝達物質」ノルアドレナリン、ノルエピレフリン、アセチルコリンなどの化学物質で、神経細胞が、ある神経刺激を他の神経細胞などに伝達する際の媒介となる物質。
Venus flytrap「ハエトリグサ」

COMPREHENSION QUESTIONS

1. [T / F] Scientists believe that a brain and nervous system are necessary for intelligence.
2. [T / F] Both Aristotle and Charles Darwin believed that a plant's root system could act like a brain.
3. [T / F] The roots of plants behave in some ways that are similar to the brains of animals.
4. [T / F] As soon as an insect lands on a Venus flytrap, the plant will close its jaws.
5. [T / F] Scientists are generally in agreement regarding plant intelligence.

USEFUL EXPRESSIONS

1. 本通りの街路樹のヤナギが新芽をふき始めた。
   The willows along the main street have (　　　　) come into leaf.
2. 科学の分野の中には、例えば量子物理学のように極度に難解で、専門家でないと理解できないようなものもある。
   Some fields of science (　　　　) quantum physics are extremely difficult for non-specialists to grasp.
3. キノコとカキはどうも私には合わない。いつも胃の調子がおかしくなるのだ。
   Mushrooms and oysters seem to (　　　　) me. They always give me an upset stomach.
4. 出生時の体重が2.5キロ未満の子は、以前はよく「未熟児」と呼ばれていた。
   Children whose birth weight is less than 2.5kg have often (　　　　) "premature infants."
5. 一方の極では食べ物を捨てる人々がいるのに、その一方で餓死する人々がいる。
   (　　　　), there are people who throw food away, while at the other, there are those who die of hunger.

---
at one extreme　　be described as　　disagree with
start [begin] to　　such as

39

WRITING

1. この薬は、腫瘍内の血流量を減らすことから、腫瘍に対して効果があるといわれている。
(it / been / drug / has / that / this / suggested) is effective against tumors as it decreases tumor blood flow.
2. ここの亜熱帯気候は日本の気候、特に沖縄の気候に似ている。
The semitropical (of / that / like / is / here / climate) Japan, especially of Okinawa.
3. 通信技術の発達のおかげで、私たちは世界中のどこのニュースでも即座に知ることができる。
Developments in communications technology have (get / made / news / to / it / possible) from anywhere in the world instantaneously.

SUMMARY

① 68

Plants may be intelligent even though they lack a brain and a (1.   ). They seem to have a sophisticated awareness of their environment and the ability to communicate. Their root system seems to act like a brain. The (2.   ) can transmit various kinds of information to other parts of the system that control the (3.   ) and direction of roots. Plants are also extremely sensitive to light. Some, such as the Venus flytrap, seem to exhibit a kind of (4.   ). Some scientists suggest that plants may be conscious and may even feel pain. But rather than saying plants are intelligent, it may be more accurate to say that they have a high level of (5.   ).

| awareness | growth | memory | nervous system | root cap |

DID YOU KNOW?

木々は私たちが考えている以上に周囲に気を配り、自分の仲間に迫り来る危険を知らせているらしい。例えば害虫に葉を食われている木はある化学物質を出して周囲の木々にその危険を伝え、周りの木々はそれ感知し虫の嫌う物質を出し始めるという。地下の根幹からは、命の元の水の状態や栄養素の有る無しなどの情報が発信されているらしい。

UNIT 11 Insecticide Resistance
耐性昆虫との闘い

耐性とは、生物が生存するために供えた能力であり、自らに悪害を及ぼす物に対して抵抗し、さらにはそれに対する免疫を獲得することである。生命体の変異と選択による進化の最も身近な一例といえる。農業の分野では病害虫の殺虫剤耐性や植物の除草剤耐性のことが話題に上ることが多いが、医学、薬理学、微生物学の分野でも薬剤耐性、薬物耐性、薬剤抵抗性などと呼ばれ、その対策が急がれている。

BASIC WORDS IN CONTEXT

1. Through the powers of biotechnology, low-nicotine tobacco, disease-resistant cotton and soy immune to weed killer are (　　　　) in Hawaii.
2. As the number of people who (　　　　) pets as part of the family increases, more people suffer psychologically when these pets die.
3. Weather forecasters are (　　　　) against a possible snowstorm in the northern part of Japan.
4. The word Jupiter originally (　　　　) "God (Ju-) the father (-piter)."
5. Her cold got worse and (　　　　) into pneumonia.

| develop | grow | mean | regard | warn |

READING

① 69〜73

CD 69 One great advantage of genetically modified (GM) crops is that they allow farmers to cut down on the amount of toxic pesticides they use. Not only does this save them money, it is also good for the environment. Bacillus thuringiensis (Bt) crops, for example, contain toxins that kill a variety of pests. In 1999, 29 million acres of Bt corn, potato and cotton were grown globally. It has been estimated that by using cotton protected with Bt, the United States alone was

5

able to save approximately $92 million.

70 But for any species, evolving and adapting to new factors in its environment is as natural as breathing. Recent analysis of the first 400 million hectares of Bt crops has shown that five out of 13 species of pest are now resistant to Bt toxins. So far, the resistance is relatively minor and confined to certain areas, and so experts generally regard this as a good result. But they warn that unless farmers take efforts to keep this resistance from evolving further, they risk losing the considerable financial benefits of Bt crops.

71 One measure is to design crops that make more than one toxin. This means that even if bugs develop resistance to one of them, the others will still kill them. Another option available to farmers is the planting of so-called "refuges." This refers to the practice of planting non-Bt crops in fields close to Bt crops. The idea is that this will create the opportunity for pests on the refuge crops to breed with any bugs on the Bt crops that have developed Bt resistance. As a result, any resistance genes that are passed on will not be expressed in the descendants.

72 The biggest problem with creating refuges is that it is expensive for farmers. In general, farmers in richer countries such as Australia and the United States have had success with this method. Farmers in poorer countries such as India or the Philippines are usually too financially strapped to use this method. Consequently, resistance has usually evolved quickly. In response to this problem, seed companies such as Monsanto and Dow AgroSciences have developed what they call "refuges in a bag." In other words, they mix Bt and non-Bt seeds together in exactly the correct proportions to give the required size of refuge. As a result, farmers do not have to create their own refuges and so find it easier to comply with the rules.

73 Insecticide resistance is a never-ending problem that requires seed companies to conduct ongoing research and development. But it is also vital that farmers follow new rules, and so new solutions must be cost-effective, even for poorer farmers.

Unit 11 – *Insecticide Resistance*

NOTES

Bt (= Bacillus thuringiensis) 「バチルス・チューリンゲンシス」殺虫効果のある病原菌 **express** 遺伝形質が表面に現れる **Monsanto**「モンサント」米ミズーリ州に本社を持つ多国籍バイオ化学メーカー。遺伝子組み換え作物の種の世界シェアは90%。**Dow AgroSciences**「ダウ・アグロサイエンス」米インディアナ州に本社を置く総合化学品メーカー「ダウ・ケミカル」の傘下にあり、殺虫剤などの農薬以外にも食物の種や生物工学溶液などの開発販売をしている。

COMPREHENSION QUESTIONS

1. [T / F] Using Bt corn, potato and cotton crops has saved the United States approximately $92 million.
2. [T / F] Experts are very worried that five out of 13 species of pest are now resistant to Bt toxins.
3. [T / F] Crops designed to contain more than one toxin will be more effective in providing a safeguard against resistance.
4. [T / F] The use of refuges is not so widespread in poorer countries.
5. [T / F] Seed companies are giving farmers financial assistance to create refuges.

USEFUL EXPRESSIONS

1. 他の組織に転移しない腫瘍は良性と呼ばれ、がんとは呼ばれない。
   A tumor that doesn't spread to other tissues is called benign, and is not (   ) as cancer.
2. テレビ界の有名人による地震被災者に対する援助の呼びかけに応じて、人々は多額の義援金を寄付した。
   People donated lots of money (   ) the appeal by TV celebrities for aid to the earthquake victims.
3. そのカマキリの色は、いわゆるオリーブドラブ（オリーブの葉の色のような、緑と茶の中間色）だ。
   The color of that praying mantis is (   ) olive drab.
4. 私は健康のために肉を食べる量を減らし、もっと野菜を食べようとしているところだ。
   I'm trying to (   ) my meat consumption and eat more vegetables for the sake of my health.
5. 感染性疾患は、細菌を含むさまざまな微生物によって引き起こされる
   Infectious diseases are caused by (   ) microorganisms, including bacteria.

   a variety of   cut down on   in response to   refer to   what they call

WRITING

1. 集中治療室にいるその患者には、近親者しか面会を許されていない。
   Only (allowed / close / to / are / relatives / visit) the patient in the intensive care unit.
2. 同じ仕事をすれば女性でも男性と同じ給料を貰う権利があるという考え方は、現在ではごく自然なことだと受け取られている。
   The idea that women deserve the same pay for doing the same work as men (quite / is / as / natural / regarded) these days.
3. 私に思いやりがなかったために、妻が重い病気にかかっていることに気が付かなかった。
   My thoughtlessness (my / kept / that / noticing / from / me) wife was seriously ill.

SUMMARY

 75

Bt crops contain (1.   ) that kill pests, but recent analysis shows that some pests are now resistant. So far, (2.   ) is minor and confined to certain areas. Farmers must take efforts to keep it from evolving further. One measure is to design crops with more than one toxin. Another is "refuges" — planting non-Bt crops close to Bt crops. This will allow (3.   ) on the refuge crops to breed with bugs on the Bt crops that have developed Bt resistance. As a result, any resistance (4.   ) that are passed on will not be expressed in the descendants. To help poorer farmers, seed companies have developed "refuges in a bag," mixing Bt and non-Bt seeds together in the correct proportions to give the required size of (5.   ).

| genes | pests | refuge | resistance | toxins |

DID YOU KNOW?

薬剤の反復投与によりその薬剤効果が薄れることはよく知られているが、これには組織耐性と代謝耐性の2つがある。組織耐性とは、薬剤が作用する受容体の数が減少するなど薬の作用点に組織レベルの変化が起きた結果、薬が効かなくなることであり、代謝耐性とは、肝臓などで薬剤を分解する酵素の産生が増強された結果、体内での薬剤濃度が減少し薬効が低下してしまうことである。どちらも生命体が自らを維持するために発達させた機能である。

UNIT 12

Unwelcome Guests

寄生

寄生は植物間（ブナとヤドリギ）、動物間（ヒトとカイチュウ）、動植物間（クリタマバチとクリ）のようにさまざまな生物間で見られるが、実は寄生と共生の間の境は明確ではないという。相利共生の例として、アリとアブラムシ、イソギンチャクとクマノミ、マメ科植物と根粒バクテリア、地衣類を構成する菌類と藻類などがよく知られているが、果たしてお互いに利する関係など存在するのだろうか。

BASIC WORDS IN CONTEXT

1. There are many good musicians in the world, but the great ones are (　　　　), not made.
2. An (　　　　) wound generally puffs up the skin surrounding it.
3. It appears that (　　　　) tops and flying kites aren't very popular activities these days.
4. Laura says she managed to (　　　　) her weight by switching to wholewheat bread with fewer carbs.
5. I bought a paperweight (　　　　) like a T-rex as a souvenir from Jurassic Park.

> bear　　control　　infect　　shape　　spin

READING

① 76〜80

76 Nature provides us with examples of interaction between species that are mutually beneficial. For instance, tiny organisms that live inside an animal's gut can aid the digestive process, while certain birds and insects, especially bees, are responsible for pollinating plants. This kind of relationship is known as symbiotic. On the other hand, we also see in nature examples of parasitic　5 behavior, where one animal (the parasite) benefits at the expense of the other (the host), in some cases causing the host's death.

77 The usual relationship between ants and aphids is symbiotic, i.e. they help each other. The aphids provide honeydew to ants, while the ants protect them from predators such as ladybugs. But just before winter sets in, a particular type of flat aphid is born. Unlike their round parents, the flat aphids emit chemicals that fool the ants into identifying them as ant larvae and carrying them back to their nests. Like vampires, the aphids ruthlessly feed on the ants' young by piercing the ant larvae and sucking out their blood. The ants have no clue that the aphids are preying on their young, and when spring comes, the ants dutifully carry them back above ground. It could be that the aphids' behavior is a strategy for getting through the cold winter weather unscathed.

78 Praying mantises have been seen to display suicidal behavior, walking to the edge of a river and throwing themselves in. Less than a minute after the mantis has entered the water, the horsehair worm Gordius emerges from its anus. This type of worm is a parasite that infects insects such as praying mantises. However, for part of its life, it needs to find another host that lives in water. To make the switch from land to water, it has developed the ability to cause its insect host to jump into a river and drown.

79 One of the most bizarre parasitic interactions takes place in the jungles of Costa Rica. This is an example of how one creature can control the mind of another, turning it into a kind of zombie. A female wasp paralyzes a spider with a sting. She then lays an egg on its body. The spider recovers and continues to build normal webs. During this period, the wasp larva hatches and feeds on the spider's bodily fluids. After a while, the larva injects a chemical into the spider that causes it to spin a differently shaped web. When this is completed, the larva kills and eats the spider. It then spins a cocoon to complete its development. The spider's new web is used to support the cocoon and protect it from being swept away by heavy rains.

80 Parasitism shows us how the battle for survival in nature can take some strange yet ingenious twists and turns.

Unit 12 – *Unwelcome Guests*

NOTES

symbiotic「共生の」 **parasitic**「寄生の」 **unscathed**「無傷で」 **horsehair worm Gordius**「ハリガネムシ」幼虫は昆虫や甲殻類に寄生した後、水中で自由生活をして産卵、再び陸上の宿主へと舞い戻る。 **twists and turns**「紆余曲折」

COMPREHENSION QUESTIONS

1. [T / F] A symbiotic relationship means that one creature helps the other but not vice versa.
2. [T / F] Aphids may be using the ants to protect themselves from cold conditions.
3. [T / F] The horsehair worm emerges from the praying mantis and kills it.
4. [T / F] The wasp that lays the egg is able to control the mind of the spider.
5. [T / F] The wasp larva forces the spider to build a shelter that will protect it.

USEFUL EXPRESSIONS

1. この地域の農民たちは寒く厳しい冬が来る前に全ての果実を収穫しなければならない。
   Farmers in this area will have to pick all the fruit before the cold, harsh winter (　　　　　　).
2. いわゆる「進歩」というものは、私たちのもろく傷つきやすい環境を犠牲にすることによってのみ達成される。
   So-called "progress" can only be realized (　　　　　　) our fragile environment.
3. 情報技術の分野は飛躍的な進歩を遂げている。
   Extremely rapid progress is (　　　　　　) in the field of information technology.
4. もし雨が降らなければ、大部分の農民たちがこの夏を乗り切れないだろう。特にこの長期間にわたる干ばつの後にはそうである。
   Unless it rains, most farmers won't be able to (　　　　　　) the summer, especially after this long dry spell.
5. メスのコンドルは2年に一度しか卵を産まないので、次の世代がアンデスの山々の上を飛び回るのを見るまでには時間がかかる。
   Female condors (　　　　　　) only every two years, so it takes time to see the next-generation condors flying over the Andes.

| at the expense of | get through | lay an egg | set in | take place |

WRITING

1. 牛やヤギは私たちにミルクを提供してくれる。
   Cows and goats (us / provide / milk / with).
2. 魔術師が呪文の言葉を言った途端、ロープがヘビに変わった。
   The moment the magician said "Abracadabra," (a / the / turned / snake / rope / into).
3. 論理が紆余曲折するので，彼の演説の流れを追うのは難しかった。
   (the / in / and / twists / his / turns / logic) made his speech difficult to follow.

SUMMARY

The relationship between aphids and ants is normally symbiotic — they help each other. One type of aphid, however, tricks the ants into thinking aphid (1.   ) are really ant larvae. When the ants carry them into their nests, the aphids feed on the ants' young and hibernate till spring. Some praying (2.   ) throw themselves into rivers and die. A horsehair worm then emerges from their anus to complete its development in water. It causes the mantis to kill itself. A (3.   ) in Costa Rica lays an egg on a spider. When the larva hatches, it injects chemicals into the spider to make it spin a web that the wasp (4.   ) can use for protection. When the spider has completed the (5.   ), the wasp larva kills it and eats it.

| cocoon | larvae | mantises | wasp | web |

DID YOU KNOW?

一生のうちに宿主を変える寄生虫にとって、宿主間の移動は大問題である。本章で紹介したハリガネムシは、カマキリやカマドウマの寄生虫として知られているが、秋になるとその宿主を水辺へ誘い水中で産卵し、カゲロウなどの水生昆虫の体内へ侵入、その中間宿主がカマキリやカマドウマに捕食されることで再び主たる宿主へ乗り移り、成体へと成長するのである。

UNIT 13 Galileo's Inclined Plane
斜塔には行かなかったガリレオ

落下する物体はどのように動くだろう。ソフトボールはゴルフボールより先に地面に到達するだろうか。アリストテレスの権威を打ち砕いたとされる鉄球の実験は、イタリアの数学者・物理学者・天文学者だったガリレオによりピサの斜塔で行われたと言われているが、果たして彼は実際にそこに行って鉄球を落したのだろうか。

BASIC WORDS IN CONTEXT

1. Only five people finished the marathon. The rest were defeated by the August heat and (　　　　　) by the wayside.
2. Many years passed before anyone (　　　　　) out Einstein's theories of relativity.
3. Today's temperature was the highest (　　　　　) this year.
4. The accidental introduction of the nonnative snake has (　　　　　) biologists' fears that a lot of other animal species might be threatened.
5. Living things are broadly (　　　　　) into animals and plants.

> divide　　fall　　increase　　record　　test

READING

② 02〜06

The Italian scientist Galileo Galilei (1564-1642) is perhaps best known as the inventor of the telescope and for his support of Copernicus's theory that Earth orbits the sun, not vice versa. But he was also intrigued by gravity. He disagreed with the accepted theory (put forward by the Greek philosopher Aristotle) that objects fall at a speed relative to their mass. His own hypothesis was that they would fall with the same acceleration, and he wanted to design an experiment to test this idea. We now know that his much-talked-of experiment of dropping two balls from the top of the Leaning Tower of Pisa is probably an old wives' tale. In fact, he used an ingenious gadget and a pencil and paper to prove his prediction.

CD 03 His biggest problem was measuring technology. At the time there was no device such as a stopwatch that could accurately record high speeds. This meant that he could not observe free-falling motion by dropping objects from a high tower because they would fall too rapidly to be measured. Galileo needed a way to slow the motion down. So, for the experiment, he constructed an inclined plane and rolled a ball down it.

CD 04 To measure the speed of the ball, he used a water clock, and to measure distance, he used a ruler divided into 60 *punti* ("points"), or roughly 60 millimeters. In the first few moments, he found that the ball rolled 33 points. After an equal amount of time, it rolled 130 points. In the end, his measurements for eight equal intervals were as follows: 33, 130, 298, 526, 824, 1,192, 1,620 and 2,104.

CD 05 These figures clearly showed that the ball was accelerating as it descended. But what was their significance? Galileo had the idea that the increases might be related proportionally to the initial figure. He therefore took the first figure of 33 and used it to divide the following figures: 130/33, 298/33, 526/33, etc. The results of these calculations were 3.9, 9.03, 15.9, 25.0, 36.1, 49.1 and 63.8. He realized immediately that these numbers were almost equivalent to squared numbers: $2^2=4$, $3^2=9$, $4^2=16$, $5^2=25$, $6^2=36$, $7^2=49$ and $8^2=64$. He therefore concluded that the distance covered increased with the square of the time. This enabled him to predict that if the ball were to continue rolling, the next factor would be $9^2=81$, and so on.

CD 06 In other words, Galileo's ingenious experiment enabled him to come to the following conclusion: if an object is released from rest and gains speed at a steady rate (for example, in free-fall or when rolling down an inclined plane), then the total distance that the object travels is proportional to the square of the time needed for that travel.

Unit 13 – *Galileo's Inclined Plane*

NOTES

Aristotle「アリストテレス（384-322 B.C.）」古代ギリシャの哲学者でプラトンの弟子。認識論・知識論の基礎となる四原因の措定、三段論法の定式化、動物の発生や分類の研究、天体論などの業績で「万学の祖」と呼ばれた。　**Copernicus**「コペルニクス（1473-1543）」ポーランドの天文学者。天文学に革命的影響を与え近代科学成立を促した。　**an old wives' tale** 非科学的な古い慣習や信仰

COMPREHENSION QUESTIONS ② 07

1. [T / F] Aristotle believed that the mass of an object determined the speed at which it falls.
2. [T / F] Galileo's experiment of dropping two balls from the top of the Leaning Tower of Pisa was a great success.
3. [T / F] Galileo rolled the ball down the plane 33 times in order to get his results.
4. [T / F] Galileo was unable to measure the speed of the ball with complete accuracy.
5. [T / F] Galileo's results enabled him to predict future results.

USEFUL EXPRESSIONS

1. 大部分の両親は子供たちにとって良い見本となり得るが、その逆はあり得ない。
   Most parents can be a good example to their children, but not (　　　　　).
2. 全ての生物は大きく動物と植物の2つに分けられる。
   All living things (　　　　　) animals and plants.
3. 近年のエネルギー危機に対処するため、次回会合の議題は次のように変更されます。
   In order to deal with the recent energy crisis, the agenda of our next meeting will be changed (　　　　　).
4. アインシュタインは時間と空間は関連していることに気が付いた。
   Einstein realized that time (　　　　　) space.
5. 最も初期のコンピューターは、計算力では現在のポケット電卓と同等だった。
   In calculating power, the earliest computers (　　　　　) modern pocket calculators.

---

as follows　　be divided into　　be equivalent to　　be related to　　vice versa

WRITING

1. 僕は化学の中間試験日に病気だったが、教授は追試を受ける機会を与えてくれた。

   I was sick (of / at / mid-term / the / chemistry / time / examination / the) but the professor let me take a make-up exam.

2. 太陽の下に長時間いて、肌をあまりにも早く焼こうとするのは良くないよ。日に焼け過ぎて痛い水ぶくれになるよ。

   It's not good for you to (to / quickly / too / sitting / try / by / tan) in the sun too long. You'll get a painful sunburn.

3. もしこの計画を協力して締め切りまでに終わらせるというのならば、我々はお互いに完全に腹を割りうそを言わないことが大切だ。

   If we (cooperate / finish / to / are / and) this project in time, it's important that we be completely frank and honest with each other.

SUMMARY ② 08

Galileo disagreed with Aristotle's theory that (1.   ) fall at a speed relative to their mass. His (2.   ) was that they would fall with the same acceleration. There was no (3.   ) then that could accurately record high speeds, so he could not observe free falling motion by dropping objects from a high tower. To slow the motion down, he constructed an inclined (4.   ) and rolled a ball down it. He used a water clock to measure the speed and a (5.   ) divided to measure distances. His figures showed that the ball was accelerating as it descended. He realized that they were almost equivalent to squared numbers. He therefore concluded that the distance covered increased with the square of the time.

| device   hypothesis   objects   plane   ruler |

DID YOU KNOW?

1971年8月2日、アポロ15号で月に着陸したDavid R. Scott 船長はガリレオの実験を無重量の中で再現した。落下する2つの物体がどのように振る舞うのかを探ろうという実験である。彼の片手にはファルコンの羽、もう一方にはハンマー。2つの物体は、スコットの手を離れると並んで落下し、1秒余り後にほぼ同時に月面に当たった。

UNIT 14 All the Colors of the Rainbow

ニュートンとプリズム実験

1672年1月、ニュートンは優れた哲学者（当時科学者はそう呼ばれていた）の団体として創立間もないロンドン王立協会へ一通の手紙を送った。彼が行った「ある哲学上の決定実験 (experimentum crucis)」は、太陽光（白色光）はそれまで考えられていたような純粋な光ではなく、異なる色の光線が混じり合ったものであることを簡単な実験で示したものだった。

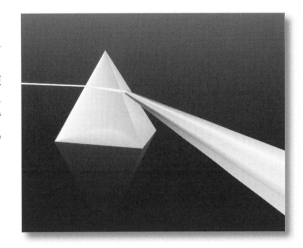

BASIC WORDS IN CONTEXT

1. Please be reminded that the garbage must be (   ) for proper recycling.
2. The faster the speed, the slower time (   ) — in other words, the slower we age.
3. I picked up my frail grandmother from her wheelchair and (   ) her on the bed.
4. In autumn the leaves on the trees in mountains everywhere (   ) red and yellow.
5. This machine (   ) a fabric 50 to 100 times finer than a spider's web.

> create   lay   pass   separate   turn

READING

② 09〜12

Isaac Newton (1643-1727) was one of the most remarkable scientific geniuses that ever lived. Working in physics, astronomy and mathematics, he made groundbreaking discoveries that laid the foundation for much of modern science. One of his greatest achievements was in the field of optics, i.e. the study of light. In Newton's time, the prevailing belief was that white light was pure and homogeneous. People certainly understood that if white light traveled through a prism, it was transformed into different colors, but they believed that the prism was somehow "staining" the light. Newton wanted to determine the true nature of light and color. The experiment he devised revealed a profound truth yet was very simple to understand and reproduce.

Newton allowed a beam of light to shine into a darkened room through a small hole in the window. It then shone through a prism onto a wall about four meters away. Newton noticed that it created a pattern somewhat resembling a rainbow. Although its shape was wrong — oblong rather than curved — it contained the horizontal bands of color from red to blue that we normally associate with a rainbow.

Newton then took a step that set him apart from his predecessors — he added a second prism. He drilled a small hole in a board and placed this prism behind it. He then passed part of the oblong band of light through this prism and directed the beam onto another board. By turning the first prism, he was able to make different colored light shine onto the second board. He made two key observations. First, the degree to which the prism refracted the different colors did not change. Second, the way they were refracted did not depend on the angle at which the light struck the prism. He thus concluded that the degree by which the rays were refracted was not a property of the prism but of the rays themselves. In other words, the prism did not modify the rays but simply sorted them according to their refractive properties in the same way that droplets of water in the air refract light to form a rainbow.

On other occasions, Newton had used additional prisms to recombine light that he had separated, finding that this recombined light is white. This led him to a conclusion that turned conventional wisdom on its head: sunlight, or white light, is not pure but is composed of rays of different colors. This discovery helped Newton to solve other problems related to light. He concluded that objects do not actually possess color, but that we perceive them as a particular color because their surface reflects one type of light more strongly than others.

NOTES

prism「プリズム」滑らかに磨いた平面を2つ以上持つ透明体のこと。分光器に用いるものの多くは三角柱。**oblong rather than curved**「湾曲しているというよりは横長の楕円形の」虹の様に曲がっているのではなく楕円状に横に延びた形をしていること

COMPREHENSION QUESTIONS

1. [T / F] Isaac Newton was most famous for his work in the science of optics.
2. [T / F] In his experiment, Newton used a prism placed outside a darkened room.
3. [T / F] Newton was not the first person to notice that a prism affected the color of light.
4. [T / F] Newton concluded that each color of light has a refractive angle that never changes.
5. [T / F] Newton's experiment confirmed what most people believed about the color of light.

USEFUL EXPRESSIONS

1. 我々の体内の全ての細胞は核と細胞質から構成されている。
   All the cells in our body (　　　　　) a nucleus and cytoplasm.
2. 汚染の度合いは、基本的には汚染物質の性質と量に基づいている。
   The degree of pollution basically (　　　　　) the nature and amount of the pollutant.
3. 最近の研究によると、「よく学びよく遊べ」はかなり当たっている。
   (　　　　　) recent research, it is quite true that all work and no play makes Jack a dull boy.
4. 彼の神経外科医としての経歴が、人工知能の分野で彼を他の研究者から際立たせている。
   His background as a neurosurgeon (　　　　　) other researchers in the field of artificial intelligence.
5. 江戸時代、脚気（かっけ）は白米しか食べないことと関係していた。
   In the Edo Period, beriberi (　　　　　) the eating of only white rice.

---

according to 　　be associated with 　　be composed of
depend on 　　set ... apart from

WRITING

1. 立て続けのフェリー事故は、これまでに起こった事故の中で最も恐ろしい災難だった。

   The successive ferry disasters (most / were / that / tragedies / frightening / the) ever happened.

2. 天候がこんなに目まぐるしく変わるのには嫌気が差すね。車のワックスがけが終わった途端また雨だ。

   (way / I / the / weather / the / hate / changes) so quickly. It starts pouring again the moment I finish waxing my car.

3. これらの悲惨な事件は世界を破滅の縁に追いやってしまうかもしれない。

   These disastrous events (might / to / the / lead / world) the very brink of destruction.

SUMMARY

② 14

In Newton's time, people believed light was pure. When a prism broke light into different colors, they thought the prism was "staining" it. Newton allowed a (1.   ) of light to shine through a prism in a darkened room and strike the wall. The image contained horizontal (2.   ) of color from red to blue. He then added a second prism and allowed the different bands of light to shine onto a board one at a time. He noticed that the (3.   ) to which the prism refracted the different colors did not change. He concluded that the angle of (4.   ) was not a property of the prism but of the rays. In other words, the prism did not modify the (5.   ) but simply sorted them according to their refractive properties.

| bands | beam | degree | rays | refraction |

DID YOU KNOW?

ニュートンはこの実験の後、次のように言っている。「哲学をする上で最高にして最も安全は方法は、まず最初に物事の性質を入念に調べ、明らかになった性質を実験によって確立し、その後それらの性質を説明する仮説へと一層時間をかけて進んでいくことのようだ」。つまり、科学者は現象を見て仮説を立てて実験を行い、真実を明らかにするまでさらに仮説を立てる作業を続けていく、ということだ。

UNIT 15

Watching the Earth Move

フーコーの振り子

19世紀初めには地球の自転が常識となりつつあったが、それを物理的に証明する方法はまだ開発されていなかった。フランス人物理学者のフーコー (Foucault) は、振り子の振動方向は赤道以外の場所では地球の自転によって、見かけ上北半球では右回りに、南半球では左回りに少しずつずれていくはずだと考えた。幾度かの実験を繰り返したフーコーは1851年、パリ天文台で公開実験を行い、成功を収めた。

BASIC WORDS IN CONTEXT

1. We are currently (　　　　　) some problems with the circuit.
2. Due to the instability of the current web server, we have (　　　　　) our website to the following address.
3. We (　　　　　) the experiment over 200 times following her procedures and got nowhere.
4. Wooden houses (　　　　　) back and forth in the big earthquake.
5. Hey presto! Now all the pain is (　　　　　).

> fix　　go　　move　　repeat　　swing

READING

② 15〜18

We all know that the Earth rotates but we are unable to see or feel this movement. The reason is that we become aware of movement only if we can see it in relation to a fixed point. If every object is moving at the same speed, then everything will appear to be still. But there is one device which allows us to see quite clearly that we live on a rotating sphere. This is the Foucault Pendulum.

The French scientist Léon Foucault (1819-1868) stumbled across it by accident. One day while working in his laboratory in Paris, he inserted a flexible metal rod into a lathe. He then "twanged" it, as one would do with a guitar string, and found that it began to move up and down in a straight line from top to bottom. (We can picture it going from the 12:00 position to the 6:00 position on a clock face, for example.) Foucault then decided to see what would happen if he rotated the chuck into which the rod was inserted by 90 degrees. To his great surprise, he found that as the chuck turned, the direction of the movement stayed the same, continuing to move between 12:00 and 6:00. Foucault repeated the experiment using a pendulum attached to the ceiling. The same thing happened. The pendulum swung in the same direction no matter which way its mounting point moved.

What causes this phenomenon is the principle of inertia, which says that a moving body will continue to move in the same direction unless an outside force acts on it. In other words, once the pendulum is set in motion, its direction of swing will not change unless it is pushed or pulled. On the other hand, the earth will rotate once every 24 hours. If you continue to watch the pendulum, you will notice that its line of swing seems to gradually move. Our common sense tells us that the pendulum is moving and the floor underneath it is stable. However, the opposite is true. The pendulum continues to move in exactly the same direction, while the room itself moves along with the rotation of the earth. The pendulum just appears to rotate.

If such a pendulum were set up at the North Pole, it would appear to rotate through a full 360 degrees in one day. This is because at this location, the earth and the pendulum do not have a great influence on one another. As you move south, however, not only is the earth rotating, it is also carrying the pendulum with it. This has the effect of slowing the rotation of the swing. When you reach the equator, the effect is so great that the pendulum does not appear to move at all. Below the equator, the movement begins again but goes in the opposite direction.

Unit 15 – *Watching the Earth Move*

NOTES

lathe「旋盤」　picture「（人が物事など）を心に描く」imagine よりも「ありありと目に浮かべる」という感じ。　chuck「（旋盤・ドリルなどの）つかみ，回転軸に固定する器具」　inertia「慣性，惰性」

COMPREHENSION QUESTIONS

1. [T / F] The Foucault Pendulum shows us that Earth rotates even though it does not appear to do so.
2. [T / F] Foucault designed his pendulum in order to demonstrate Earth's rotation.
3. [T / F] No matter how Foucault changed the mounting point, the swing of the pendulum stayed the same.
4. [T / F] The movement of the pendulum is determined by the law of inertia.
5. [T / F] The pendulum will move in exactly the same way at the North and South Poles.

USEFUL EXPRESSIONS

1. 医師たちが可能な治療法について論議している間にも，その患者の体力は弱り続けていた。
   The doctors argued over possible treatments, while the poor patient (　　　　　　) weaken.
2. 実験マウスの取り違えは、偶然ではなく故意に起こったに違いない。
   The mix-up of the experimental mice must have happened not (　　　　　　), but by design.
3. 血中に溶け込んだグルコースは、空腹感を生じさせる重要な役割を果たしているようだ。
   The glucose dissolved in the blood (　　　　　　) play a crucial role in eliciting hunger.
4. 1975年、2人の若者が車庫の中にコンピューターを作る会社を立ち上げた。
   In 1975, the two young men (　　　　　　) shop in a garage to make computers.
5. ダーウィンの進化論は出版されるとすぐに急速に広まった。
   Darwin's theory of evolution (　　　　　　) rapidly gain ground soon after it was published.

---

appear to　　begin to　　by accident　　continue to　　set up

WRITING

1. 循環中の血液はその全てが5分に1回腎臓を通過する。
   The total volume of circulating blood passes (the / five / kidneys / through / every / once / minutes).

2. 気象学者たちはかねてより超大型ハリケーンがフロリダを襲ったらどんなことになるかを指摘し、説明してきていた。
   Meteorologists have long pointed out and described (hit / what / a / happen / would / mega-hurricane / if) Florida.

3. 前立腺がん患者が増えたのは、西欧風の生活習慣が普及したためだという人もいる。
   Some people say that the (reason / cancer / in / prostate / the / increase / for) is the spread of the Western lifestyle.

SUMMARY

We are not aware that Earth is moving, because we cannot see that it moves in relation to a fixed point. However, the Foucault Pendulum shows us that Earth rotates. Foucault discovered this by accident. In his (1.   ), he "twanged" a rod and found that it moved up and down. No matter how he changed the point where the rod was mounted, it continued to move in the same direction because of the (2.   ) of inertia. When the (3.   ) is set in motion, its line of swing appears to gradually move. We think the pendulum is moving and the floor is stable, but in fact the opposite is true. The pendulum moves in the same (4.   ), while the room moves along with the (5.   ) of the Earth.

| direction | laboratory | pendulum | principle | rotation |

DID YOU KNOW?

幼いころから機械仕掛けが好きだったフーコーは科学医になろうと医学を学び始めたが、血を見たり人が苦しむのを見たくない自分に気付き医学の道を諦めた。やがて彼の興味は同じフランス人のルイ・ダゲールが開発した写真術に向かい、鮮明な太陽の撮影や光の絶対速度の測定、さらには望遠鏡に用いる鏡の製作など現代科学の礎の構築に大いに貢献した。

UNIT 16

The G Factor

知能とは何だ？

「知能」と「知性」はどう違うのだろうか。従来「知能」とは答えのある問いに対して素早く正確な答えを出す能力のことであり、「知性」とは答えの無い問いに対して決して諦めず、時には生涯をかけて問い続ける力であるとされてきた。だが「知能」と「知性」の間に果たして明確な線引きができるのだろうか。

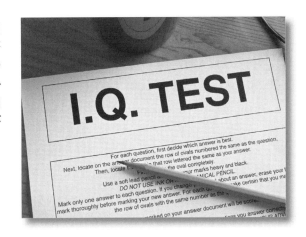

▶ BASIC WORDS IN CONTEXT

1. Some roses are (　　　　　　) after such celebrities as Ingrid Bergman, Elizabeth Taylor, and Judy Garland.
2. That new theory on the origin of our universe has still been (　　　　　　) by only a few scholars.
3. It may be a great honor for Mt. Fuji to be registered as a World Heritage site, but it will be quite a job to (　　　　　　) it properly.
4. Among scientists, it's commonly (　　　　　　) that a virus is the cause of cancer.
5. Infectious diseases are caused by a variety of microorganisms, (　　　　　　) bacteria.

| accept | believe | include | name | preserve |

▶ READING

② 21〜24

21 What is intelligence? In the early 20th century, British psychologist Charles Spearman noticed that people who do well on one kind of mental test also do well on others. He came to the conclusion that all such tests measure a deep general ability, which he named "the g factor." Other experts, however, believed that multiple forms of intelligence exist, including verbal skill and spatial awareness.

22 In 1993, the U.S. psychologist John B. Carroll put forward a now widely accepted theory that united both views. He proposed a three-tier structure of intelligence, shaped like a pyramid. At the top is a single cognitive ability — a general intelligence factor called "g." Under that, there are eight broad abilities. All of these contain "g," but also have other elements that make people stronger in certain specific areas. These elements include visual or auditory perception, and the speed at which information can be processed or retrieved. Below these are 64 narrower abilities. All of these contain the elements in the first two levels but also include more general factors such as life experience and specialized aptitudes.

23 Another question that has sparked a lot of debate is whether intelligence is fixed or whether it can change throughout our lifetime — for better or worse. Some researchers make a distinction between what they call fluid intelligence (gF) and crystallized intelligence (gC). The former relates to general abilities such as reasoning and problem solving, whereas the latter relates to the "crystallized" results of our former learning, such as proficiency in our native language and broad cultural knowledge. While we are young, these two abilities run neck and neck, but gF abilities decline as we age, perhaps because our brain's ability to process information slows down. On a brighter note, however, age does not seem to affect gC abilities in most people. In the workplace, for example, this means that older workers may not be able to solve new problems so quickly, but they will be able to use their large reserves of knowledge and experience.

24 There are supplements and drugs available, such as steroids, to increase our muscle mass, but currently, there is no substance available that will boost our intelligence. Some people use caffeine or nicotine to increase their alertness, but these substances have no permanent effect on our intelligence, and long-term use may well be dangerous to health. There has also been a lot written about the positive effects that so-called "superfoods" — oily fish, avocadoes, blueberries, broccoli, etc. — can have on our cognitive abilities. But there is no reliable scientific evidence to back these claims. Until intelligence-enhancing drugs are developed — if such a thing is even possible — the best way to preserve our intelligence into old age is the tried and tested approach of living a healthy life: taking physical exercise, eating a balanced diet and getting sufficient sleep.

Unit 16 – *The G Factor*

NOTES

three-tier structure「3層構造」　**steroid**「ステロイド」脂肪溶解性の有機化合物の総称　**caffein(e)**「カフェイン」コーヒー・茶などに含まれるアルカロイド。強心剤や利尿剤としても使われる。　**nicotine**「ニコチン」タバコの葉に含まれるアルカロイド。神経を刺激または抑制する作用がある。　**back**「〜を支援・支持する」

COMPREHENSION QUESTIONS ② 25

1. [T / F] Charles Spearman was an expert who performed very well on mental tests.
2. [T / F] John B. Carroll's work brought together two different views of intelligence.
3. [T / F] Crystallized intelligence does not develop until we are older.
4. [T / F] Older workers can be of value because of their gC abilities.
5. [T / F] A combination of steroids and superfoods may improve our mental alertness.

USEFUL EXPRESSIONS

1. 免疫機能が維持されていれば、エイズ患者も適度に普通の生活を送ることができる。
   People with AIDS (　　　　　) be able to live a reasonably normal life if their immune system is maintained.
2. 狭いケージで飼われているペットには、体重の管理やストレス発散のために運動をさせることが大切だ。
   It's important for pet animals kept in small cages to (　　　　　) in order to control their weight and release stress.
3. 良くも悪くも、人類は核エネルギーを使うことを学んでしまった。
   (　　　　　), humans have learned to use nuclear energy.
4. 3つのトップグループがiPS細胞の研究開発にしのぎを削っていた。
   Three top groups were (　　　　　) in research and development of iPS cells.
5. 残念なことに、梅雨は母の関節炎に悪い影響を及ぼしているようだ。
   Unfortunately, rainy weather seems to (　　　　　) my mother's arthritis.

```
for better or worse    have ... effect on    may well
         run neck and neck    take exercise
```

WRITING

1. 大都市のマンションの中には、他人の迷惑にならない限り居住者がペットを飼うことが許されているところもある。

    In some condominiums in big cities, residents can keep pets as long as (one / bother / not / others / does / the).

2. 温帯地域では毎年、春と冬が訪れる—前者は花を伴い、後者は雪を伴って。

    In the temperate zones, spring and winter come every year; (its / the / with / flowers / former) and (latter / its / the / snow / with).

3. 食生活の変化のせいだろうか、小麦の消費が増える一方でコメの消費が減りつつある。

    Probably due to the change in diet, consumption of wheat is on the rise, (that / rice / whereas / of / declining / is).

SUMMARY

We now use a three-tier structure of (1.   ). At the top is a general intelligence factor called g. Under that, there are eight broad abilities such as visual or auditory (2.   ), and the speed at which you process or retrieve information. Below these are 64 narrower (3.   ). Fluid intelligence (gF) relates to reasoning and problem solving while crystallized intelligence (gC) relates to results of former learning. gF abilities decline as we age but gC abilities remain. Currently, no (4.   ) is available to boost our intelligence. Until intelligence-enhancing drugs are developed the best way to preserve our intelligence into old age is to live a healthy life: taking physical exercise, eating a balanced (5.   ) and getting sufficient sleep.

| abilities | diet | intelligence | perception | substance |

DID YOU KNOW?

知性とは一般的には物を考えたり判断したりする能力のことだとされるが、意志や感情、推理によらない直観的認知能力のことも指すといわれている。いずれにしても、物事の真理や対象物の存在を前にしたときの精神の力のことだろう。

UNIT 17

A Trip to the Land of Nod
眠りの不思議

人は一晩に1時間半の眠りを4、5回繰り返すという。それぞれの眠りは、浅い眠り2回、深い眠り2回、浅い眠り1回の後に急速眼球運動 (Rapid Eye Movement = REM) を伴った眠りで構成される。この最後の REM の間に人は夢を見るといわれている。

BASIC WORDS IN CONTEXT

1. The news of her untimely, sudden death (   ) to all of us like a bolt from the blue.
2. Small dietary changes, including more fiber and dairy, can (   ) reduce the risk of colon cancer.
3. Last night I thought I hit upon a brilliant idea, but after having (   ) on it, I'm not so sure.
4. We (   ) our trip to Timbuktu, though we had to put up with a good deal of inconvenience.
5. The Slow Food movement is aimed at (   ) not only what we eat but how we live.

> change   come   enjoy   help   sleep

READING

② 27〜31

27 Even though we spend roughly one third of our lives sleeping, there is still a lot we do not know about it. Normal adults need between seven and nine hours' sleep a night. This seems a lot considering how busy we are and how many distractions are available to us. But scientists have discovered that skimping on sleep comes at a high cost. Sleeplessness has been linked to a rise in obesity and diabetes, and around 20 percent of traffic accidents are linked to fatigue. A 17-year study in Britain focused on 10,000 civil servants who cut their sleep from seven hours to fewer than five. It found that they were 1.78 times more likely to die from all causes. Specifically, their risk of dying from cardiovascular disease went up 2.5 times.

[28] Why do we need sleep? Several reasons have been suggested. It helps regulate the activities of our autonomous nervous system, such as heart rate. It could also help consolidate memories by reducing the amount of information traveling through our nervous system. It may even help us consolidate the rules of our complex human social lives.

[29] Some people suffer from sleep disorders. Sleep apnea syndrome is a condition that causes pauses in breathing or shallow or infrequent breathing during sleep. Apnea sufferers are not usually aware they have this condition, but two potential signals are excessive, loud snoring and drowsiness or fatigue during the day. Another, often quite embarrassing, sleep disorder is narcolepsy. It occurs when the brain is unable to regulate periods of sleep and wakefulness. People with narcolepsy experience excessive drowsiness during the daytime and may suddenly fall asleep at any time no matter what they are doing.

[30] The most common sleep disorder, however, is insomnia. It is estimated that it causes around $60 billion in damages to U.S. businesses every year. Various types of medication are available for people who find it difficult or impossible to nod off. They work by mimicking the mechanisms of natural sleep, targeting neurotransmitters and receptor sites in the brain. Most of them are effective, but not a silver bullet. Sleep follows a very strict structure of five or six cycles, each lasting about 1.5 hours, in which rapid-eye-movement sleep follows non-rapid-eye-movement sleep. Sleep medication can disrupt these cycles, as well as our brainwaves, leaving us feeling somewhat groggy when awakening.

[31] It may be possible in the future to develop more sophisticated sleeping drugs that allow us to sleep and wake whenever we want with no ill effects. This would allow us to truly enjoy the benefits of our 24/7 society, as well as avoid jet lag. But we should be aware that our basic biological mechanisms have not changed much over hundreds of thousands of years as a species, so fooling them will not be an easy job.

Unit 17 – *A Trip to the Land of Nod*

NOTES

distractions「気晴らし，娯楽」 **cardiovascular disease**「心臓血管系の病気」 **sleep apnea syndrome**「睡眠時無呼吸症候群」 **narcolepsy**「ナルコレプシー」昼間突然耐え難い眠気を催し眠りに陥ってしまう睡眠発作 **insomnia**「不眠症」 **silver bullet**「問題解決の特効薬，確実な解決法」magic bullet とも言う。 **24/7** (=24-7)「24時間年中無休の」

COMPREHENSION QUESTIONS

1. [T / F] Between seven and nine hours a night is the recommended sleeping time for normal adults.
2. [T / F] Our heart rate plays an important role in regulating sleep.
3. [T / F] Narcolepsy is a sleep disorder that causes loud and excessive snoring.
4. [T / F] U.S. businesses spend $60 billion a year trying to find a cure for insomnia.
5. [T / F] Sleeping medication that enables us to sleep and wake whenever we want to with no ill effects is not yet available.

USEFUL EXPRESSIONS

1. 音が空中を伝わる速さは気温により変化する。
   The speed of sound (　　　　　) the air varies according to the temperature.
2. 中国には優に180万頭もの羊がいるが、それはオーストラリアとニュージーランドの羊を足した数よりずっと多い。
   In China, there are no (　　　　　) 1.8 million sheep, which is a far greater number than those in Australia and New Zealand put together.
3. 地震とそれに続く津波で被害を受けた全て人々のことを考えると、胸が痛みます。
   My heart bleeds for everyone who (　　　　　) the earthquake and the subsequent tsunami.
4. いつもはいとも簡単に寝つくのですが、昨夜は大変でした。多分コーヒーを飲み過ぎたせいでしょう。
   Although I usually (　　　　　) quite easily, I had a hard time last night probably because I drank too much coffee.
5. 2000年というごく最近、世界中でおよそ77万7,000人の子供たちが麻疹（はしか）で亡くなったことを知っていますか。
   Did you know that some 777,000 children (　　　　　) measles worldwide as recently as in 2000?

| die from | fall asleep | fewer than | suffer from | travel through |

WRITING

1. 大学入学時には、学費がこんなに急に上がるなどとは夢にも思っていませんでした。
   When I started college, I never dreamed that there (this / in / rise / rapid / tuition / be / would).
2. 我々の中には危なくなどないと思っている人が多いのだろうが、また山の遭難記事が新聞に出ていた。
   (was / an / another / there / accident / article / about) on the mountain, even though many of us may think that it poses no danger.
3. 地上高く綱渡りをしている人を見るたびにとても不安になる。
   I get extremely nervous (see / I / whenever / walking / someone) on a tightrope high up above the ground.

SUMMARY

Scientists have discovered that skimping on sleep is dangerous. It is linked to a rise in obesity and (1.   ). People who cut their sleep from seven hours to fewer than five were 1.78 times more likely to die from all causes. Sleep (2.   ) include apnea, a condition that causes pauses in breathing during sleep. Another is narcolepsy, which causes excessive daytime (3.   ). The most common is (4.   ). Sleep medication mimics the mechanisms of natural sleep. Most are effective, but not a silver bullet. Sleep medication can disrupt natural sleep cycles and brainwaves, leaving us feeling groggy when awakening. We may one day invent sleeping drugs that allow us to sleep and wake whenever we want with no ill (5.   ).

> diabetes   disorders   drowsiness   effects   insomnia

DID YOU KNOW?

睡眠は心身の休息、細胞レベルでの自然治癒、記憶の再構成などに深く関わっているとされているが、人は成長に伴いそれぞれ異なった眠りのパターンを取る。新生児は短時間の睡眠を断続的に多数回取り、1日に16時間も眠るが、2歳児になるとこれが9〜12時間に減り、成人では6〜9時間になる。高齢になると昼間に何度も居眠りし、夜間は数時間しか眠れないというパターンになるのが普通だ。

UNIT 18

Lab-Grown Organs

再生医療

再生医学は、胎児期にしか形成されない人体の組織に欠損が起きた場合にその機能を回復させる医学分野だ。その手法にはクローン技術、臓器培養、多機能性幹細胞の利用、自己組織誘導などがある。本章にも紹介されているが、将来的には豚などの体内や人の体内で臓器を養殖するという手法も研究されている。

BASIC WORDS IN CONTEXT

1. I wonder how much gas is wasted by those who rev their engines while (　　　　　) for the lights to change.
2. Quite recently, a lot of doctors, young and old, have (　　　　　) into alternative medicine.
3. The problem seemed simple at first glance, but I soon realized that there was more to it than (　　　　　) the eye.
4. Beliefs of the older generation are (　　　　　) in low esteem by many young people today.
5. More and more farmers are trying to market their produce themselves instead of (　　　　　) established distributors.

| get | hold | meet | use | wait |

READING

② 34～40

34 Since the first human transplant operation was carried out in 1967, transplant surgery has become safer and more widespread. But not everyone who needs a transplant can get one. The main problem is that there are simply not enough transplantable organs available. And even if an organ is available, there is always a risk that the recipient's body will reject it.

35 But a solution may be on the horizon since scientists now have the ability to grow new organs in the laboratory. Until recently, the focus has been on creating relatively simple organs such as windpipes, blood vessels and parts of the larynx. These bioengineered organs have been successfully transplanted into humans. But scientists were doubtful that they could create more complex organs such as the heart, liver or lungs.

There has now been a huge breakthrough. For the first time ever, scientists have taken a kidney grown entirely in a laboratory and successfully transplanted it into a rat. This rat kidney is the most sophisticated organ yet created outside of the body. Based on this success, it is conceivable that other complex organs could also be grown in the same way.

One great advantage of bioengineered organs is that the chances of the recipient rejecting the new organ are very small. This is because the technique used to produce them gets rid of all the donor's cells. The organ in question is washed with a mild detergent until all that remains is a basic scaffold structure. This is made of collagen, an inert protein that the recipient is unlikely to reject. Scientists then regrow the flesh of the organ by seeding this scaffold with cells taken from the recipient.

Currently there are more than 100,000 people in the United States on the waiting list for a kidney, but only 18,000 kidney transplants are performed each year. This breakthrough is certainly good news for people in this situation and it could undoubtedly save many lives. But it will still not provide enough kidneys. We could meet the entire demand, however, if we were able to harvest organs from animals. When considering the size of human organs, the most likely animals to use would be pigs, though some people might find this a step too far.

Even though lab-grown organs hold out great promise, many problems remain before they can be widely used. When transplanting an organ, one of the main complications is the amount of time needed to attach it to the recipient's body. Once the operation starts, blood has to reach each cell as soon as possible. If not, cells that do not receive oxygen will start to die. Some U.S. researchers are trying to solve this problem by growing new organs inside a patient's body.

Through these ingenious pioneering approaches, the future may be brighter for the many people on the long waiting lists for transplant surgery.

NOTES

windipes「気管」 **blood vessels**「血管」 **larynx**「喉頭，発声器官」 **scaffold structure**「足場，土台となる組織」 **collagen**「コラーゲン」 **seed**「接種する」 **harvest organs from animals**「動物から臓器を摘出する」

COMPREHENSION QUESTIONS

1. [T / F] Receiving a new organ does not necessarily guarantee a successful outcome for the patient.
2. [T / F] Scientists are considering the possibility of transplanting a lab-grown kidney into a rat.
3. [T / F] If a bioengineered organ is very small, the recipient may reject it.
4. [T / F] Bioengineered organs contain no original cells from the donor.
5. [T / F] Pigs could potentially provide organs for humans because they would be the right size.

USEFUL EXPRESSIONS

1. タンパク質は細胞の全てのプロセスを制御するアミノ酸の結合体で、基本機能を担っています。
   Proteins are the bundles of amino acids that control all cellular processes, (   ) basic functions.
2. クローン科学者は卵細胞から核を取り出し、それをクローン化される動物から取り出された細胞の核と入れ替えるのです。
   Cloning scientists remove the nucleus from an egg cell, and replace it with one from a cell (   ) the animal to be cloned.
3. もし発熱やけいれん、下痢などの症状が出たら、なるべく早く病院へ行ってください。
   If you experience symptoms such as fever, cramps or diarrhea, please see a doctor (   ).
4. 遺伝医学の新しい発見により、遺伝性疾患の中にもいつの日か治癒できるものが出てくるかもしれないという希望が出てきている。
   New discoveries in genetic medicine (   ) the hope that some hereditary diseases may one day be curable.
5. 近所で見つけたその迷い犬に愛着を感じ始めたため、見捨てることは到底できなかった。
   I've become so (   ) that stray puppy I found in my neighborhood that I can't just abandon it.

| as soon as possible | attach to | carry out | hold out | take from |

WRITING

1. 問題は、極北のこの地域から南へ数千キロ離れた消費者まで石油を運ぶことだ。
   (gas / problem / sending / is / the / from) this region in the far north to consumers several thousand kilometers away down south.

2. 全てのネールサロンの技術者が適切なまつげエクステンション施術を行えるかどうか怪しいものだ。
   (it's / artists / that / nail / all / doubtful / the / salon) are capable of giving proper eyelash extension treatment.

3. 魚を食べることは卒中にかかる可能性を減らすという証拠がある。
   There is evidence that fish consumption (reduces / of / having / chances / the) a stroke.

SUMMARY

It is now possible to grow new (1.) in the laboratory. One advantage of bioengineered organs is that (2.) are unlikely to reject them because the technique used to produce them gets rid of all the (3.) cells. The organ is washed until all that remains is a basic scaffold structure made of an inert (4.) that the recipient is unlikely to reject. Scientists then regrow the flesh of the organ by seeding this scaffold with cells taken from the recipient. More than 100,000 people in the United States are waiting for a kidney, but only 18,000 kidney (5.) are performed each year. We could meet the entire demand if we could harvest organs from animals. For humans, the most likely animals would be pigs.

| donor's | organs | protein | recipients | transplants |

DID YOU KNOW?

移植適合性や拒否反応など臓器移植医療の持っている難点を克服する手法として、再生医学には大きな期待が寄せられている。特に人工多機能性幹細胞 (iPS細胞) は世界の注目を浴びており、今後の研究の進展が待たれる。

UNIT 19 Looking for New Earths
新しい地球を探せ

地球外生命が存在する可能性は高いと推測される一方で、彼らとの接触が皆無であるという矛盾は「フェルミのパラドックス」と呼ばれている。銀河の直径は 10 万光年。光速の 1,000 分の 1 で銀河を端から端まで旅したとすると、約 1 億年かかることになる。その銀河では中性子星の崩壊などによるガンマ線爆発が数百万年に一度起き、生命は根絶やしになるという。宇宙を旅することができるほどの高度の知能を備えた生命が地球に到達するには、数百万年というこの時間はあまりにも短い。

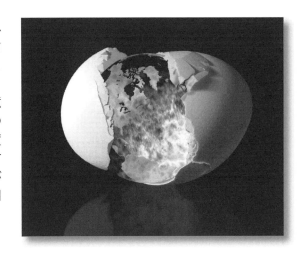

BASIC WORDS IN CONTEXT

1. I had thought that (　　　　　) in the countryside would be pleasant, but after only two months, I was completely fed up.
2. The threatening weather gave us second thoughts about (　　　　　) on our hike early this afternoon.
3. No effective treatment for cancer of the pancreas has been (　　　　　).
4. Scientific conclusions must be (　　　　　) on solid research conducted through rigorous procedures.
5. How (　　　　　) to come down with the flu right in the middle of our long-awaited vacation!

> base　disappoint　establish　live　start

READING

② 43〜47

CD 43　Extraterrestrial life, as depicted in science fiction movies, generally resembles some form of life found on Earth, such as humans, lizards or insects. But such complex creatures actually represent only a small part of life on Earth. The creatures that dominate our biosphere are much simpler, single-celled creatures such as bacteria and archaea, many of which live under rock and ocean beds. If we find life beyond Earth, it is likely that this is the kind of life it will be.

44 The first question is to decide where to look. The best way to start is by searching for planets with an environment similar to that of Earth, with a surface temperature of between 0 and 100°C as well as abundant water. They should also receive solar radiation to promote photosynthesis and be geologically stable. Using NASA's Kepler telescope, scientists have established that there may be millions of Earth-sized planets in the so-called habitable zone around their parent stars. It therefore makes sense to investigate the closest ones.

45 Life on Earth is based on the unique bonding properties of the carbon atom, but it is quite conceivable that if there is life elsewhere in the universe, it will not be carbon-based. This means that we have to develop ways of looking for properties that are common to all life forms, no matter what their chemical composition may be. One key property is that life creates dynamic interactions. In other words, life forms extract energy and raw materials from their environment and release waste products. This has the effect of changing their surroundings. For example, photosynthesis has completely changed the way Earth looks, and the CO_2 in Earth's atmosphere fluctuates on an annual cycle. If scientists detect changes such as these in a planet, this could indicate the presence of life there.

46 But how is it possible to identify what is happening in the atmosphere of distant planets? Scientists have discovered that starlight shining through a planet's atmosphere can give us information about its chemical composition. We have already started to analyze the temperature and chemical make-up of Earth-type planets. NASA's launch of the James Webb Space Telescope (scheduled for 2018) will make this job easier since it is able to measure the temperature of planets as well as search for signs of substances that are crucial to life, such as water, oxygen, nitrogen, ozone and methane. Eventually, it may also help us to detect seasonal cycles and other changes that may be evidence of life.

47 Science fiction fans may be disappointed that our first encounter with extraterrestrial life is unlikely to involve pointy-headed creatures emerging from a spaceship. But finding any kind of life, no matter how small, will change the way we look at the universe and, more importantly, at ourselves.

Unit 19 – *Looking for New Earths*

NOTES

archaea「古細菌」メタン菌、高度好塩菌、好熱好酸菌、超好熱菌など。極限環境に生息する。単数形はarchaeon。**James Webb Space Telescope**「ジェームズ・ウェッブ宇宙望遠鏡」米航空宇宙局（NASA）が中心となり開発中の赤外線宇宙望遠鏡。ハッブル宇宙望遠鏡の後継機として2018年以降に打ち上げ予定。

COMPREHENSION QUESTIONS

1. [T / F] If we discover extraterrestrial life forms, they are more likely to be simple than complex.
2. [T / F] In our search for extraterrestrial life, we should look at planets where the water temperature is less than 100°C.
3. [T / F] Life on Earth as we know it would not exist if it were not for carbon atoms.
4. [T / F] We would be more likely to find life on a planet with a stable atmosphere than a changeable one.
5. [T / F] The James Webb Space Telescope has provided us with valuable information about other planets.

USEFUL EXPRESSIONS

1. インターネットで何かを探すことには、かなり当てずっぽう的な側面がある。
   (　　　　　) things on the Internet is pretty much hit or miss.
2. 手術の後、母は思ったほどは回復しなかった。
   After her operation, mother didn't recover (　　　　　) expected.
3. どんな薬を投与しても、その少年の熱はなかなか下がらなかった。
   The boy's temperature wouldn't go down (　　　　　) medicine he was given.
4. 研究者たちによれば、脂肪分の多い食品はインスリン生成に必須のGnT-4aという酵素の働きを抑えることがあるという。
   According to researchers, fatty foods can suppress the enzyme GnT-4a, which (　　　　　) the production of insulin.
5. 鳥を捕らえたりネズミのような小動物を狩ることは、ネコに共通の欲求である。
   The desire to hunt birds and small animals such as mice (　　　　　) cats.

| as well as | be common to | be crucial to | no matter what | search for |

WRITING

1. 知識人であると同時に行動派であることは可能だろうか。
   (is / it / possible / to / be) a man of letters and a man of action at the same time?
2. 体重を減らす最良の方法は、食べる量を減らすことである。
   (to / best / weight / take / the / way / off) is to reduce the amount of food you eat.
3. 恐らく充分に考えられるのは、我々が実験で用いた手順で重大な間違いを犯したことだ。
   (conceivable / suppose / I / quite / it's) that we've made a serious mistake in the procedures used in the experiment.

SUMMARY

If we find life beyond Earth, it is likely to be single-celled (1.   ). We have to search for planets with an environment similar to that of Earth. There may be millions of Earth-sized planets, so we should investigate the closest ones. Life elsewhere in the (2.   ) may not be carbon-based, so we have to look for (3.   ) common to all life forms. Scientists have discovered that starlight shining through a planet's (4.   ) can tell us about its chemical (5.   ). We have already started to analyze the temperature and chemical make-up of Earth-type planets. NASA's James Webb Space Telescope will make this job easier since it can measure the temperature of planets and search for signs of crucial substances.

| atmosphere | composition | creatures | properties | universe |

DID YOU KNOW?

疑似科学と言われる説の中には、宇宙人の存在に関するものが数多く存在する。例えば、米ネバダ州のグルーム・レイク空軍基地「エリア51」には墜落した宇宙船と宇宙人が保存されているが、米政府は彼らとのコンタクトを否定し軍事機密にしているという話は「インデペンデンス・デイ」や「Xファイル」などの映画にもしばしば出てくる。

UNIT 20 Weird and Wonderful Worlds

月がとっても多いから

「月」は「ある惑星から見てその周りを回る衛星」を指し、例えば「フォボスは火星の月の1つである (Phobos is one of Mar's moons.)」のように表現する。月の模様はさまざまに解釈されるが、古代中国や日本ではウサギが餅つきをしているといい、西欧ではカニの姿とか編み物をする老婦人と見たり、ネイティブアメリカンや北米、東欧では女性の顔と見る慣習がある。

BASIC WORDS IN CONTEXT

1. When (　　　　　) to themselves, Japanese usually point at their noses, while Americans point at their chests.
2. STAP cells turned out to be a hoax, and the scientific community was (　　　　　) with a red face.
3. Rescue parties were (　　　　　) to the disaster-stricken area, where over 5,000 inhabitants were in a state of panic.
4. Lots of insects that (　　　　　) the piercing-cold winter started to stir.
5. Mt. Pinatubo (　　　　　) enormous quantities of ash into the atmosphere.

> emit　　leave　　point　　send　　survive

READING

Until around 400 years ago, we knew of only one moon in our solar system — the one we see in our own night sky. Then Galileo pointed his telescope in the direction of Jupiter and found four more. Since then, we have continued to discover new moons. There are currently around 20 times more named moons in the solar system than planets. These moons are far from similar to each other. In fact, they are remarkably diverse, and some scientists claim that some of them may even have the necessary conditions for supporting certain forms of life.

Titan, one of Saturn's moons, has sometimes been described as "the second Earth." It has lakes, hills, caves, river valleys, muddy plains and desert sand dunes. Its atmosphere contains fog, mist and rain clouds. On seeing images of it for the first time in 2005, one scientist joked that it looked just like England! But even though England may be cold, it is not as cold as Titan, where the surface temperature reaches a maximum of minus 180 degrees Celsius. Some researchers believe that its lakes contain chemicals that could be a source of food for life.

Io, one of Jupiter's moons, is so cold that it is permanently covered in layers of sulfur dioxide frost. Despite this, it is the most volcanic world we know. Its surface area is one-twelfth that of Earth, but it produces 100 times as much lava as all Earth's volcanoes put together. Some of Io's eruptions send plumes of gas and dust soaring up more than 500 kilometers.

Jupiter's moon Europa and Saturn's moon Enceladus are both icy yet very active. Scientists have suggested that they may even provide environments where living creatures could survive. Europa's elliptical orbit means that Jupiter's gravitational pull on it strengthens and weakens, making its rocks flex. This stress warms the moon from within, enough to maintain a watery ocean below the surface. Possible hydrothermal vents could supply nutrients to support microorganisms. On Enceladus, geysers emit jets of water vapor and ice crystals. Some of this falls back to the surface as snow, making this moon the whitest object in the solar system.

One of the strangest moons is Nereid, which belongs to Neptune. Instead of gently circling its planet like other moons, it swoops steeply in and out. At its furthest point, it is nine million kilometers from Neptune, but it then plunges back to within 1.4 million kilometers of it. Moons with irregular orbits are generally thought to be former comets or asteroids captured by a planet's gravity. The composition of Nereid, however, is different from such objects, leaving its origin shrouded in mystery.

Unit 20 – *Weird and Wonderful Worlds*

NOTES

Celsius「セ氏」スウェーデンの天文学者セルシウス(A. Celsius)が考案した温度目盛り。欧米ではこれに対しドイツの物理学者ファーレンハイト(G. D. Fahrenheit)の作ったカ氏を用いているところが多い。 FとCの関係は F= 9/5 C+ 32。

COMPREHENSION QUESTIONS

1. [T / F] Galileo was the first person to discover a moon that did not belong to Earth.
2. [T / F] Saturn's moon Titan has physical features that resemble those of Earth.
3. [T / F] Io has 100 times as many volcanoes as Earth.
4. [T / F] Even though it is very cold, Jupiter's moon Europa has a watery ocean on its surface.
5. [T / F] Neptune's moon Nereid behaves like a former comet but has a different composition.

USEFUL EXPRESSIONS

1. その医師は私の息子が、私の知る範囲で何らかの薬にアレルギーがあるかどうか知りたがっている。

   The doctor wants to know if my son is allergic to any kind of medication that I (   ).

2. その薬は、僕には全く何の助けにもならなかった。それどころか、かえって悪くなったようだ。

   The medicine didn't help me at all. (   ), I'm afraid I'm even worse off.

3. 今私たちが火星に立っているとして、あなたは地球はどのように見えると思いますか。

   If we were standing on Mars, what do you think Earth would (   )?

4. ライオンやトラのようなどう猛な動物がネコの仲間（ネコ科）とは信じられない。

   I can't believe that fierce animals like the lion and the tiger (   ) the cat family.

5. 夜眠れないときは、羊の数ではなく幸福なことの数を数えるようにしてみたら。

   If you can't sleep at night, try counting your blessings, (   ) counting sheep.

---

belong to   in fact   instead of   know of   look like

WRITING

1. その奇っ怪な生き物を見るやいなや，私はそれこそ必死で逃げた。
   (creature / the / on / strange / seeing), I ran as if my life depended on it.
2. 確かにここは最近はずっと寒かったですが、アラスカの寒さとは比べ物になりません。
   It certainly has been cold here lately, but (nothing / it's / as / like / cold) as Alaska.
3. 夜は気温が下がるので、植木を屋内ポーチに運ばなければならない。
   It (that / gets / I / night / so / at / cold) have to bring the plants onto the porch inside the house.

SUMMARY

There are around 20 times more moons in the solar system than planets. These moons are diverse, and scientists claim that some may be able to support (1.   ). Saturn's moon Titan has (2.   ) that resemble those of Earth. The maximum surface temperature is minus 180 degrees Celsius. Its lakes contain (3.   ) that could be a food source for life. Jupiter's moon Io is the most volcanic world we know, producing 100 times as much (4.   ) as all Earth's volcanoes. Jupiter's moon Europa and Saturn's moon Enceladus are both icy yet very active. Scientists have suggested that they may even provide (5.   ) where life could survive. Neptune's moon Nereid does not gently circle its planet like other moons. Instead, it swoops steeply in and out.

> chemicals   environments   features   lava   life

DID YOU KNOW?

女性が月を見ることを禁忌とした言い伝えは、世界各地にある。イヌイットの伝承では「娘が月を見ると妊娠するから見てはいけない」とか、アイスランドでは「妊婦は月に顔を向けてはいけない。子供が精神障害になるからだ」とか、北欧では「妊娠した女は月を見てはいけない」など、月と妊娠や月と精神障害を結びつけた禁忌は多い。lunatic や loon(e)y のような言葉にも、それが残っている。

UNIT 21 The Invisible Universe

見果てぬ宇宙

古くは「とおめがね」と呼ばれた望遠鏡は、遠くにある物体が発する可視光線・赤外線・X線・電波などの電磁波を捉えて観測する装置だ。電磁波の「波長」によって光学望遠鏡と電波望遠鏡に、電磁波を「捉える方法」により反射望遠鏡と屈折望遠鏡に大別される。

BASIC WORDS IN CONTEXT

1. My mother's breast cancer was (　　　　) in the early stages, so the surgery was relatively simple.
2. This over-the-counter medicine doesn't seem to (　　　　) for my bad cough. I need to see a doctor.
3. The 21st century has (　　　　) remarkable changes in the field of medical science.
4. During the experiment, we dealt with each of the difficult problems as they (　　　　).
5. I know how to satisfy my sweet tooth without (　　　　) my waistline.

> arise　　detect　　expand　　witness　　work

READING

② 57〜61

The human eye is an extremely sophisticated organ, but it can detect only a certain portion of the electromagnetic spectrum, responding to wavelengths from about 390 to 750 nanometers. This means that even with the help of powerful optical telescopes, we can see only a tiny fraction of the universe. Most of it, as far as the naked eye is concerned, is invisible.

58 In 1800, the British astronomer William Herschel was the first to detect invisible radiation. This was in the infrared range (740 nanometers to one millimeter). Infrared astronomy became widely used in the 1960s. Most infrared radiation is absorbed by water and CO_2 in the atmosphere, and so infrared telescopes work best from space. Infrared astronomy allows us to study comets and asteroids, as well as the interstellar medium, the most important source of infrared light that reaches Earth. It is a mixture of gas and dust in the space between stars. Observations of interstellar dust have allowed us to witness the birth and death of stars and planetary systems.

59 What is more, infrared radiation is essential for understanding the universe. NASA discovered that more than half of the energy from distant stars begins life at optical and ultraviolet wavelengths. This is absorbed by dust and emitted again in the infrared part of the spectrum before it reaches us. It can also help us to "look back in time" and understand how galaxies first arose. This is possible because the universe is expanding, and so most galaxies are traveling away from us. That means the radiation they emit undergoes a Doppler shift, or "red shift," to longer wavelengths. As a result, visible light from distant galaxies in the first billion years after the big bang reaches us at infrared wavelengths.

60 Astronomical observation is also possible with different wavelengths. Radio and microwave telescopes are used to study the longest electromagnetic wavelengths, some of which are from the coldest objects in the universe. One major discovery made with this equipment was the background radiation from the big bang, known as cosmic microwave background, or CMB. Measurements of CMB suggest that only 4 percent of the universe is ordinary matter, while 23 percent is dark matter, probably made of unknown particles. The other 73 percent is dark energy, of which we know nothing.

61 X-ray and gamma-ray astronomy use the most energetic electromagnetic waves with wavelengths of one nanometer or less. These show us the universe in its hottest and most violent state. They can capture evidence of gas at temperatures of hundreds of millions of degrees, as well as mysterious objects such as white dwarfs, neutron stars and black holes.

Unit 21 – *The Invisible Universe*

NOTES

nano-「10億分の1」 **interstellar medium**「星間物質」水素とヘリウムを主とする星間ガスと星間塵（じん）から成る物質で銀河系の恒星間に生じる。 **Doppler shift**「ドップラー偏移」遠ざかる音がドップラー効果により低くなるのと同じように、遠ざかる光源から発せられた光（可視光線だけではなく、全ての波長の電磁波を含む）のスペクトルが長波長の方向（可視光線では赤の方向）にずれる現象。赤方偏移ともいう。 **white dwarf**「白色矮星（わいせい）」星の進化の最終段階と考えられ密度が極めて高く、地球規模の大きさの中に太陽とほぼ同じ質量が詰め込められているような星。 **background radiation** (cosmic microwave background = CMB)「背景放射線」天球上の全方向からほぼ等方的に観測されるマイクロ波のこと。

COMPREHENSION QUESTIONS

1. [T / F] There are certain wavelengths in the electromagnetic spectrum that our eyes cannot perceive.
2. [T / F] The astronomer William Herschel invented infrared radiation in 1800.
3. [T / F] Interstellar dust is responsible for the birth and death of stars.
4. [T / F] Infrared astronomy can allow us to look back at the history of the universe.
5. [T / F] We know nothing of dark matter, which makes up 73 percent of the universe.

USEFUL EXPRESSIONS

1. 炭水化物は、主にグルコースの形で腸から人間の体内に吸収される。
   Carbohydrates (   ) the human body through the intestine, mainly in the form of glucose.
2. おまえはお月さまのことを全然分かってないんだね。おとぎ話に出てくるようなものと違って、月はグリーンチーズでできてはいないんだよ。
   You are dead wrong about the moon, son. Despite what you may read in fairy stories, it's not (   ) green cheese.
3. 最先端の研究技術に習熟することが必須です。なぜなら、それが提供してくれる正確さと速さが、あなたたちには必要だからです。
   It (   ) be familiar with cutting-edge research technology because you need the accuracy and speed it provides.
4. 科学者は研究から長期間遠ざかっていると、勘を取り戻すのが難しい。
   If scientists have (   ) their research studies a long time, it's difficult for them to regain their touch.
5. 進行性の肝不全の結果、私たちの先生は入院した。
   (   ) the progressive liver failure, our teacher was admitted to the hospital.

---
as a result of   be absorbed by   be away from   be essential to   be made of
---

WRITING

1. 火星と金星は肉眼で見えますが、天王星と海王星は肉眼では見えません。
   Mars and Venus (eye / be / can / the / seen / naked / with), but Uranus and Neptune cannot.
2. 大学院生は昔は、新しく出版された学術誌が図書館に届くと、われ先に読もうと争ったものだ。
   Graduate students used to fight to (the / be / to / first / read) a newly published journal when it arrived in the library.
3. このfMRIの画像は、患者の脳のある部分はよく機能している一方、他の部分はあまりよく機能してはいないことを示している。
   This fMRI shows that some parts of the patient's brain are functioning quite well, (while / it / other / not / parts / are / of).

SUMMARY

② 63

Infrared astronomy allows us to study comets and asteroids and the interstellar medium. This is a mixture of gas and dust in the space between stars. Observing this allowed us to witness the birth and death of stars and planetary systems. Infrared (1.   ) can also help us to "look back in time" and understand how (2.   ) first arose. Visible light from distant galaxies in the first billion years after the (3.   ) reaches us at infrared wavelengths. One major (4.   ) made with radio and microwave telescopes was the background radiation from the big bang, known as cosmic microwave background, or CMB. X-ray and gamma-ray astronomy show us the universe in its hottest and most violent state, e.g. white (5.   ), neutron stars and black holes.

| astronomy | big bang | discovery | dwarfs | galaxies |

DID YOU KNOW?

20世紀に入り、電子工学の発展は望遠鏡に附属する観測装置の開発を早めた。暗視カメラ、紫外線やX線を感知するカメラ、雑音信号を消し去ることのできる冷却CCDカメラなどにより、私たちは100％に近い光子を検出できるようになった。電波望遠鏡も誕生し、宇宙空間に常駐する宇宙望遠鏡へと発展した。さらにニュートリノ望遠鏡、重力波望遠鏡等が誕生し、これで全ての波長に対する観測装置が整ったことになる。

UNIT 22

Eating Bugs

虫喰う人々

日本でもイナゴのつくだ煮、カワゲラやトビケラのつくだ煮、ハチの幼虫などを食べる「昆虫食」は今でも行われているが、世界を見てもアジア29 カ国、南北アメリカ 23 カ国、アフリカ 36 カ国で昆虫が食べられており、世界で食用に供される昆虫の数は 1,400 種に上るといわれている。これからの食糧不足に、昆虫は今後も役に立ってくれるのだろうか。

▶ BASIC WORDS IN CONTEXT

1. When alcohol is (　　　　　), it is absorbed rapidly into the bloodstream from the stomach.
2. The grasshopper, unable to see beyond the end of his nose, (　　　　　) all summer while the ants worked.
3. Nowadays it's hard to (　　　　　) a time when people weren't expected to live more than 50 years.
4. It is often said that the more rain we get in the summer, the fewer crops we (　　　　　) in the fall.
5. The earliest computers barely had the equivalent (　　　　　) power of the hand-held calculators of the early 80s.

| calculate | consume | harvest | imagine | play |

▶ READING

② 64〜69

Human beings are happy to eat two- or four-legged animals, but most of us would draw the line at consuming creatures with six legs — insects, that is. But a recent report by the U.N. Food and Agriculture Organization (FAO), suggests that switching to an insect-based diet may be a very effective way to guarantee future food security since insects contain protein, vitamins and minerals. What is more, they are cheap to produce and have environmental benefits.

65 Producing protein from animals is not efficient. Animals are fed on crops, and a lot of energy that goes to produce those crops is wasted. The FAO has calculated that it takes 10 kg of feed to produce 1 kg of beef, but only 1.7 kg of feed to produce 1 kg of crickets. By eating insects, we would at the same time get a greater yield for each kilogram of grain, need less agricultural land and create less pollution. It is no surprise, then, that some people view insects as the superfood of the future.

66 But things are not as simple as they seem. One obstacle to the adoption of a bug-based diet is the so-called "yuck factor." Even though insects are considered a delicacy in some parts of Asia, Africa and Latin America, most people in the West feel their stomachs turn at the idea of putting insects in their mouth. But human beings are by nature adaptable, and it is possible to imagine that we could eventually come to embrace an insect-based diet.

67 As well as this psychological problem, there will also be practical problems to solve. One is how to secure a plentiful supply of insects. If demand goes up, harvesting insects from the wild could end up doing away with certain species. Not only that, but we have no way of knowing what wild insects have been eating, and they could be full of harmful microbes or environmental pollutants. The only safe and secure way to get a plentiful supply of insects is to farm them as we do with the other animals we raise for food. In Thailand, for instance, about 20,000 cricket farms sprang up over a 15-year period.

68 Another fruitful approach has been suggested. Rather than feed insects to people, they could be used as food for livestock. Chickens, for example, already eat them as part of their diet in the wild. This would help the environment by reducing the pressure for more land to grow crops for animal feed. Insects could also play another environmentally important role. Researchers are looking into feeding them on waste products from industrial bakeries or breweries.

69 So whether we eat insects or not, it seems highly likely they will play a part in meeting our increased demand for food in the future.

NOTES

U.N. Food and Agriculture Organization (FAO)「国連食糧農業機関」国連の専門機関の一つで、世界の食糧生産・分配の改善・生活向上を通して飢餓の撲滅を達成するのを使命としている。 **yuck factor**「不快感を催すもの」

COMPREHENSION QUESTIONS

1. [T / F] Insects contain protein but lack vitamins and minerals.
2. [T / F] Insects are very effective at converting the food they eat into protein.
3. [T / F] Many people in the West have adapted to eating insects in their diet.
4. [T / F] There has been a large growth in the number of cricket farms in Thailand.
5. [T / F] One way that insects are useful is that they eat a large amount of waste from industrial bakeries and breweries.

USEFUL EXPRESSIONS

1. 私は本当は生命工学が好きではないことが分かり、生物工学を諦め人工知能へ鞍替えした。
   I realized that I didn't actually like biotechnology, and so I gave it up and (   ) artificial intelligence.

2. コアラはなぜ、有毒で繊維質で油分の多いユーカリの葉だけを常食にしているのだろうか。
   I wonder why koalas (   ) poisonous, fibrous and oily eucalyptus leaves only.

3. 極辛のタイ・カレーはすさまじく辛かったので、最後には味の感覚を全て無くしてしまった。
   The super-hot Thai curry was so tremendously spicy that I (   ) losing my sense of taste altogether.

4. インスタント食品のおかげで、料理をするために台所に長時間立っている必要がなくなった。
   Instant foods have (   ) the need for standing for long hours cooking in the kitchen.

5. 今日では、公害問題をないがしろにするメーカーは、非難を浴びることを覚悟しなくてはならない。
   Nowadays manufacturers who ignore the problem of pollution must be prepared to take (   ) criticism.

---

a lot of   do away with   end up ...ing   feed on   switch to

WRITING

1. 新しいコンピューターソフトを使い始める時には、内容を学ぶのにしばらく時間がかかる。
   When you first start using new computer software, (a / it / to / while / takes / learn) what's what.
2. フラウ・アインシュタインは、アルバートを偉大な科学者としてよりも大事な息子だと感じていた。
   Frau Einstein conceived of Albert as a loving son (scientist / than / great / a / rather).
3. ボトル入り飲料水ではなく水道水を飲むと金の節約になる。それだけではなく、その方がずっと環境に優しい。
   Drinking tap water rather than bottled water will save you money. (only / is / but / not / that / it) much more environmentally friendly.

SUMMARY

② 71

Insects contain protein, vitamins and (1.   ). They are cheap to produce and have environmental benefits. Eating them may be a way to guarantee future food (2.   ). While insects are a (3.   ) in Asia, Africa and Latin America, people in the West would be uncomfortable eating them. But humans are adaptable, and we can imagine that we could eventually get used to an insect-based diet. Harvesting insects from the wild could threaten the survival of some species. The only way to get a plentiful (4.   ) is to farm them. Another approach has been suggested. Rather than eating insects, we could use them as food for (5.   ). Researchers are also looking into feeding them on waste products from industrial bakeries or breweries.

| delicacy | livestock | minerals | security | supply |

DID YOU KNOW?

昆虫は、少ない飼料で生育可能な動物性タンパク質源として有望であり、将来人類が宇宙に長期滞在するときの食料としても研究されている。栄養学的には、例えばガのさなぎや幼虫では乾燥重量の半分以上がタンパク質で、ミネラルにも富む。加熱すれば雑菌などの問題もなくなる。生態学的には、昆虫が食べた植物のエネルギーを体質量に変換するとその効率は平均40％で、魚類の10％や恒温動物の1〜3％に比べて、はるかに優れている。昆虫は効率の良い動物性タンパク質の供給源となり得る。

UNIT 23

Bacterial Batteries

シュワネラ菌で発電する

電流発生菌は私たちの周りの至る所に生息しているという。その一つがシュワネラ菌だ。これらの微生物を用いた太陽電池や燃料電池は、餌となる有機物にパン工場の廃棄物やビール工場の廃液などを利用し廃棄物処理装置としての役割も担わせることができるので一挙両得だ。廃棄物の分解処理と同時に、発電が可能になるのだから。

BASIC WORDS IN CONTEXT

1. Baby teeth begin to be (   ) by permanent teeth at about age five.
2. I'm (   ) by the distinctive melodies of the ethnic music in Okinawa.
3. All animals instinctively have a drive to (   ) their own species.
4. People 40 years of age or over are also (   ) to have a stomach examination at the annual checkup.
5. Over the past few years, genetic science has (   ) much new ground.

| attract   break   conserve   replace   require |

READING

② 72〜75

As our supplies of fossil fuels such as coal, oil and gas diminish, what will we use to replace them? One candidate that has attracted a lot of attention is bioenergy, or energy from living organisms. When people hear this term, they usually think of plant-derived fuel such as ethanol, which can be used to power motor vehicles. But recent research seems to show that biofuels such as

ethanol may play only a very limited role in satisfying our future energy needs. One of the problems with this type of bioenergy is that it is an inefficient way to use land. This is because growing the crops (e.g. corn or sugar cane) required to produce it would drastically reduce the amount of land needed for growing food
5 or forest required for carbon storage and for conserving biodiversity.

73 But there is now a new potential form of bioenergy that is attracting a great deal of attention — the bio-battery, which involves using bacteria to produce clean energy from sources such as human and animal waste. In a bio-battery, the bacteria live near the anode (negative terminal). As these bacteria
10 break down organic substances, they strip away electrons. These electrons can then flow to the cathode (positive terminal), enabling the fuel cell to power an electronic device. Until recently, scientists believed that such fuel cells required extra chemicals to carry the electrons from the microbes to the anode. Because such chemicals are expensive and poisonous, bio-batteries were considered
15 impractical.

74 A recent discovery has given scientists greater confidence that a viable bio-battery can be produced. *Shewanella oneidensis* is a type of bacteria found in deep ocean sediments and soil. When they are exposed to heavy metals such as iron or manganese, they have the amazing property of being able to create
20 electric currents. Unlike human beings, these microorganisms can survive without oxygen. Instead, they "breathe" rocks. In other words, they get their energy from the combustion of molecules from minerals that they take into their cells' interior. What interests scientists is a side product of this reaction. As the cells take in these molecules, they create a flow of electricity that can
25 be directed across the outer membrane of the bacteria. In nature, this would be delivered to the rocks. In a fuel cell, however, it could flow to a graphite electrode.

75 Researchers have discovered that proteins use metal centers — known as hemes — to conduct electrons through their electrically insulated structure.
30 These hemes act in a similar way to stepping-stones that allow people to cross a river. Currently, bio-batteries are not strong enough for most practical applications, but scientists are hoping that if they can better understand the electron transfer mechanism that bacteria use, they may be able to design special proteins to make bio-batteries an efficient source of sustainable power.

Unit 23 – *Bacterial Batteries*

NOTES

Shewannella oneidensis「シュワネラ・オネイデンシス」糖や酢酸などの有機物を分解して電子を放出する菌　**manganese**「マンガン」金属元素の１つ

COMPREHENSION QUESTIONS

1. [T / F] Growing crops specifically for biofuel will negatively affect other important uses of land.
2. [T / F] Bio-batteries have the ability to transform waste products into useable electrical energy.
3. [T / F] In a bio-battery, bacteria transmit electrons from the positive terminal to the negative terminal.
4. [T / F] *Shewanella* bacteria use electrical power to move from one place to another.
5. [T / F] Scientists are confident that *Shewanella* bacteria will be widely used in future bio-batteries.

USEFUL EXPRESSIONS

1. 春が巡って来ると、また家の大掃除や衛生のことを考える時期になる。
   When spring rolls around, it's time to (　　　　　) housecleaning and hygiene again.
2. もう少し減量するには食事の量を少し減らさなければならない。
   I've got to cut down a little on (　　　　　) food I eat in order to lose some more weight.
3. ハチや鳥は花から花へ花粉を運ぶことで、生態系で重要な役割を果たしている。
   Bees and birds play an important role in ecological systems as they (　　　　) pollen (　　　　) flower (　　　　) flower.
4. 消防隊員たちは福島第一原発で超高度レベルの放射線にさらされた。
   The firefighters (　　　　　) an extremely high level of radioactivity at Fukushima No. 1 Nuclear Power Station.
5. 鉄分は一部の植物を食べることで我々の体内に取り込まれるが、もっと効果的には肉や魚を食べることで摂取される。
   Iron is (　　　　　) our body through the consumption of some plants, but more efficiently through eating meat or fish.

| be exposed to | carry ... from ... to | take into | the amount of | think of |

WRITING

1. 公平に利用できるということは、障害者が健常者と同じ「普通の」生活を享受できるということを意味する。
   To provide equal access means to (live / disabled / enable / the / to) the same "regular" lives as healthy people.
2. 電解質を補給するスポーツドリンクと違い、栄養ドリンクは糖分やカフェイン、その他の刺激物により脈拍を速めようとするものである。
   (sports / electrolytes / unlike / which / drinks / restore), energy drinks seek to quicken the pulse with sugar, caffeine and other stimulants.
3. 一部の科学者たちが興味を感じているのは、夢を見ている時に私たちの脳がどのように機能しているのかということである。
   (what / is / interests / scientists / some) the way our brain functions when we are dreaming.

SUMMARY

② 77

Bio-batteries use bacteria to produce clean energy from human and animal (1.). (2.) living near the anode break down organic substances. Electrons can then flow to the cathode to power an electronic device. When *Shewanella* bacteria are exposed to heavy (3.), they create a flow of electricity that can be directed across the outer membrane of the bacteria. In a fuel cell, this could flow to a graphite electrode. These bacteria use metal centers to conduct electrons in a way that is similar to stepping-stones. Bio-batteries are currently not strong enough for practical (4.), but scientists are hoping to better understand the electron transfer (5.) in the bacteria. This will enable them to design special proteins to make bio-batteries an efficient power source.

| applications | bacteria | mechanism | metals | waste |

DID YOU KNOW?

シュワネラ菌は、深海の海底火山の近くから採取された。クリーンエネルギーの旗手として期待される太陽光発電の分野で、最近非常にユニークな研究として注目を集めているのが、植物や光合成をする能力を持った微生物と、有機物を分解して電子を放出する能力を持ったシュワネラ菌などの微生物を組み合わせて発電させようという考えだ。

24 UNIT
Carbon Capture and Storage
二酸化炭素回収・貯留

二酸化炭素回収・貯留 (CCS) とは、気体として大気中に放出される直前または放出されたばかりの二酸化炭素を回収し、地中や水中などに封じ込めることを指す。二酸化炭素回収にはさまざまな方法があるが、現在研究が推進されている代表的なものを本章で紹介する。

BASIC WORDS IN CONTEXT

1. The new drug proved to have such dangerous side effects that the FDA has (　　　　　) its sale.
2. I had my appendix (　　　　　) at a nearby clinic at age 8.
3. Some children cried out at the top of their lungs when they were (　　　　　) with flu vaccine.
4. In the experiment, we stimulated the frog's nerve with electricity to see how it would (　　　　　).
5. From time to time people living in big cities are (　　　　　) with feelings of loneliness.

> inject　overcome　react　remove　stop

READING

② 78～82

Climate scientists generally agree that if average global temperatures rise by more than 2°C, the world will face serious consequences, including natural disasters and agricultural failures. To prevent this, we need to reduce the amount of CO_2 that we pump into the atmosphere. Increased adoption of alternative energy sources will certainly help, but they are highly unlikely to replace fossil fuels entirely. If we cannot stop producing large volumes of CO_2, then one solution is to try to contain it rather than to let it escape into the air. This is the idea behind carbon capture and storage (CCS).

79 A huge amount of CO_2 is produced by combustion in power plants or large factories. Using CCS technology, devices can be fitted to remove CO_2 from exhaust gases before they are emitted. One way this can be done is by bubbling exhaust gas through chemicals called amines. These chemicals react with CO_2 and capture it. The amines can then be heated to release the CO_2 and reused. Currently, other more sophisticated technologies are also under development.

80 This, however, is only the first stage of the process. Once the CO_2 has been captured, it must then be transported and stored. Because the volumes of liquid containing the CO_2 will be enormous, the only practical way to transport it is by using the same methods as for oil and gas — pipelines or ships.

81 Eventually the CO_2 will be injected into porous rock, where it can be kept safe for thousands of years. Scientists are confident that the technical problems involved in doing this can be overcome. But a bigger problem may be dealing with public concern about safety. Very few communities are willing to have storage sites located near them because of worries about CO_2 leaking from the ground. This means that governments will have to develop undersea storage sites. But engineers are confident that safe transportation and storage is possible. They point out that natural CO_2 has been trapped in the ground for tens of millions of years, and the technology for transporting, injecting and monitoring the gas can be copied directly from the oil and gas industry.

82 One large obstacle at the moment is cost. CCS technology and infrastructure will be extremely expensive. At present, national governments and organizations such as the E.U. are helping to implement CCS with financial subsidies and supporting policies. Norway, for example, has used the revenue from a high carbon tax to help successfully implement CCS projects in offshore gas fields. But the key to the future success of CCS will be to make it an attractive investment for the private sector.

NOTES

amine「アミン」溶解したCO_2の吸着に使われる塩基性化合物　　**porous rock**「多孔質岩石」
CO_2の貯留保存に用いられる。

COMPREHENSION QUESTIONS

1. [T / F] A 2°C rise in the average global temperature has resulted in natural disasters and agricultural failures.
2. [T / F] Technology using amines allows CO_2 to be captured and reused.
3. [T / F] Techniques for transporting and storing CO_2 can be copied from the oil and gas industry.
4. [T / F] People are generally unwilling to have CO_2 storage sites located close to the places where they live.
5. [T / F] The private sector is currently making large investments to create CCS infrastructure.

USEFUL EXPRESSIONS

1. その実験は再考の必要がある。この方法では何の成果も上げられないよ。
   We (　　　　　) rethink the experiment. I'm afraid this approach won't lead us anywhere.
2. 天気予報によれば、しばらくは雨は降りそうにない。
   According to the weather forecast, it (　　　　　) rain for a while.
3. ティミーは燃えさかる納屋に閉じ込められてしまったが、ラッシーのおかげで事なきを得た。
   Timmy (　　　　　) the burning barn, but Lassie saved the day.
4. 登山家は、高くそびえ立つ峰々を征服するためなら自らの命を危険にさらすことをいとわない人たちだ。
   Mountain climbers (　　　　　) risk their lives in order to conquer lofty peaks.
5. 専門家たちはこれまでに、密閉した部屋でこれらの石油ストーブを使うことの危険性を指摘してきている。
   Experts have (　　　　　) the danger of using these kerosene heaters in a closed room.

| be unlikely to | be trapped in | be willing to | need to | point out |

WRITING

1. もし冬眠する動物が心拍数、新陳代謝、体温を下げなければ、数カ月もの厳しい寒さを生き残ることはできないだろう。
   (it / not / were / if / for) the lowering of their heart rates, metabolism and body temperatures, hibernating animals could not survive months of bitter cold.

2. 我々は、培養菌を保管している研究室に光が入らないように細心の注意を払っていた。
   We were very careful (not / enter / light / let / to / any) our laboratory where we kept cultured bacteria.

3. 汚染のためにやがて人類は滅びるのかどうかの質問には誰も答えられない。
   Whether (pollution / not / destroy / or / eventually / will) mankind is a question that nobody can answer.

SUMMARY

② 84

If average global temperatures rise by more than 2°C, the world will face serious (1.   ). If we cannot stop producing large volumes of CO_2, then we must contain it using carbon capture and storage (CCS). A huge amount of CO_2 is produced by (2.   ) or large factories. Using CCS technology, CO_2 can be removed from (3.   ) before they are emitted. Eventually it will be injected into porous rock to keep it safe for thousands of years. Very few (4.   ) want storage sites located near them because of worries about CO_2 leaking from the ground. This means that governments will have to develop undersea storage sites. Engineers are confident that safe (5.   ) and storage are possible.

| communities | consequences | exhaust gases |
| transportation | power plants | |

DID YOU KNOW?

火力発電所や製鉄所などの廃ガスから高濃度のCO_2を回収し貯留する技術には、吸着剤に吸着させる物理吸着法、吸収液に溶解させる化学吸収法、吸収液に高圧で吸着させる物理吸収法、透過膜で分離する膜分離法、極低温で液化させた後に沸点の違いを利用して分ける深冷分離法の5つがある。そのように処理したCO_2は地中貯留、中層溶解、海底貯留などの方式で、大気中に漏れ出ないように封印されるのである。

SUMMARY
生物資源・環境関係名詞リスト

A
abilities	(Unit 16)
applications	(Unit 23)
archeology	(Unit 9)
Arctic	(Unit 6)
astronomy	(Unit 21)
atmosphere	(Unit 19)
awareness	(Unit 10)

B
bands	(Unit 14)
bacteria	(Unit 23)
beam	(Unit 14)
behavior	(Unit 5)
big bang	(Unit 21)
boards	(Unit 9)

C
cells	(Unit 3)
chemicals	(Unit 20)
cocoon	(Unit 12)
collapse	(Unit 4)
composition	(Unit 19)
communities	(Unit 24)
consequences	(Unit 24)
crater	(Unit 4)
creatures	(Unit 19)

D
degree	(Unit 14)
delicacy	(Unit 22)
descendants	(Unit 1)
device	(Unit 13)
diabetes	(Unit 17)
diet	(Unit 16)
direction	(Unit 15)
disability	(Unit 7)
discovery	(Unit 21)
disorders	(Unit 17)
donor	(Unit 18)
droughts	(Unit 6)
drowsiness	(Unit 17)
dwarfs	(Unit 21)

E
effects	(Unit 17)
energy	(Unit 9)
environments	(Unit 20)
eruption	(Unit 4)
evolutionary theory	(Unit 1)
exhaust gases	(Unit 24)
experiment	(Unit 1)
explanations	(Unit 7)
extraterrestrials	(Unit 9)

F
fake	(Unit 8)
fault	(Unit 4)
features	(Unit 20)

G
galaxies	(Unit 21)
genes	(Unit 11)
goldmine	(Unit 3)
growth	(Unit 10)

H
hemisphere	(Unit 6)
hoax	(Unit 7)
hypothesis	(Unit 13)

I
income	(Unit 8)
insights	(Unit 3)
insomnia	(Unit 17)
intelligence	(Unit 16)

J
jet stream	(Unit 6)

L
laboratory	(Unit 15)
landslides	(Unit 4)
larvae	(Unit 12)
lava	(Unit 20)
legends	(Unit 8)
life	(Unit 20)
livestock	(Unit 22)

M
mantises	(Unit 12)
mechanism	(Unit 23)
memory	(Unit 10)
metals	(Unit 23)
microbes	(Unit 5)
minerals	(Unit 22)
mutation	(Unit 2)

N
nervous system	(Unit 10)
nutrients	(Unit 3)

O
objects	(Unit 13)
observations	(Unit 7)
occurs	(Unit 9)
offspring	(Unit 2)
organs	(Unit 18)
organisms	(Unit 3)
orphanage	(Unit 7)

97

P

pattern	(Unit 9)
pendulum	(Unit 15)
perception	(Unit 16)
pests	(Unit 11)
plane	(Unit 13)
phenomenon	(Unit 1)
plasticity	(Unit 1)
poison	(Unit 5)
power plants	(Unit 24)
principle	(Unit 15)
properties	(Unit 19)
protein	(Unit 18)

R

rays	(Unit 14)
recipients	(Unit 18)
refraction	(Unit 14)
refuge	(Unit 11)
released	(Unit 9)
reports	(Unit 8)
resistance	(Unit 11)
root cap	(Unit 10)
rotation	(Unit 15)
ruler	(Unit 13)

S

scarcity	(Unit 2)
security	(Unit 22)
sighting	(Unit 8)
species	(Unit 2)
storage	(Unit 5)
substance	(Unit 16)
supply	(Unit 22)
survival	(Unit 2)

T

tactics	(Unit 5)
temperature	(Unit 6)
toxin	(Unit 11)
transplants	(Unit 18)
transportation	(Unit 24)

U

universe	(Unit 19)

W

wasp	(Unit 12)
waste	(Unit 23)
web	(Unit 12)

BASIC WORDS IN CONTEXT
基本動詞リスト

A

accept	(Unit 16)
affect	(Unit 4)
appear	(Unit 9)
arise	(Unit 21)
attack	(Unit 5)
attract	(Unit 23)

B

base	(Unit 19)
bear	(Unit 12)
become	(Unit 7)
begin	(Unit 6)
believe	(Unit 16)
bite	(Unit 7)
block	(Unit 5)
break	(Unit 23)
breathe	(Unit 1)
bring	(Unit 8)
bury	(Unit 4)

C

calculate	(Unit 22)
catch	(Unit 2)
cause	(Unit 8)
change	(Unit 17)
close	(Unit 10)
come	(Unit 17)
concern	(Unit 6)
conserve	(Unit 23)
consider	(Unit 4)
consume	(Unit 22)
control	(Unit 12)
create	(Unit 14)

D

detect	(Unit 21)
determine	(Unit 3)
develop	(Unit 11)
disappoint	(Unit 19)
discover	(Unit 7)
divide	(Unit 13)

E

eat	(Unit 1)
emit	(Unit 20)
enjoy	(Unit 17)
establish	(Unit 19)
evolve	(Unit 2)
exist	(Unit 3)
expand	(Unit 21)
explain	(Unit 8)

F
face	(Unit 6)
fall	(Unit 13)
fix	(Unit 15)
fly	(Unit 9)
form	(Unit 9)

G
get	(Unit 18)
go	(Unit 15)
grow	(Unit 11)

H
harvest	(Unit 22)
help	(Unit 17)
hold	(Unit 18)

I
imagine	(Unit 22)
include	(Unit 16)
increase	(Unit 13)
infect	(Unit 12)
inject	(Unit 24)

L
lack	(Unit 10)
lay	(Unit 14)
leave	(Unit 20)
live	(Unit 19)

M
make	(Unit 5)
mean	(Unit 11)
meet	(Unit 18)
move	(Unit 15)
multiply	(Unit 3)

N
name	(Unit 16)
nurse	(Unit 7)

O
offer	(Unit 9)
overcome	(Unit 24)

P
pass	(Unit 14)
play	(Unit 22)
point	(Unit 20)
possess	(Unit 10)
present	(Unit 1)
preserve	(Unit 16)
process	(Unit 10)
produce	(Unit 4)

R
react	(Unit 24)
record	(Unit 13)
regard	(Unit 11)
remove	(Unit 24)
repair	(Unit 3)
repeat	(Unit 15)
replace	(Unit 23)
report	(Unit 9)
reproduce	(Unit 2)
require	(Unit 23)
ride	(Unit 3)
rise	(Unit 6)

S
seem	(Unit 5)
send	(Unit 20)
separate	(Unit 14)
shape	(Unit 12)
sleep	(Unit 17)
slip	(Unit 1)
spend	(Unit 2)
spin	(Unit 12)
start	(Unit 19)
state	(Unit 4)
steal	(Unit 5)
stop	(Unit 24)
stretch	(Unit 1)
suggest	(Unit 8)
survive	(Unit 20)
swing	(Unit 15)

T
take	(Unit 8)
test	(Unit 13)
think	(Unit 2)
touch	(Unit 10)
turn	(Unit 14)

U
use	(Unit 18)

W
wait	(Unit 18)
warn	(Unit 11)
warm	(Unit 6)
wear	(Unit 7)
witness	(Unit 21)
work	(Unit 21)

USEFUL EXPRESSIONS & WRITING
基本熟語・慣用表現・構文リスト

A

a lot of	(Unit 22)
a rise in	(Unit 17)
a variety of	(Unit 11)
according to	(Unit 14)
all over	(Unit 7)
allow ... to	(Unit 11)
another	(Unit 17)
appear to	(Unit 15)
as a result (of)	(Unit 21)
as ... as	(Unit 20)
as far as	(Unit 4)
as follows	(Unit 13)
as soon as possible	(Unit 18)
as such	(Unit 4)
as well as	(Unit 19)
at least	(Unit 9)
at one extreme	(Unit 10)
at the expense of	(Unit 12)
at the time of	(Unit 13)
attach to	(Unit 18)

B

be absorbed by	(Unit 21)
be associated with	(Unit 14)
be away from	(Unit 21)
be common to	(Unit 19)
be composed of	(Unit 14)
be connected to	(Unit 6)
be crucial to	(Unit 19)
be described as	(Unit 10)
be divided into	(Unit 13)
be equivalent to	(Unit 13)
be essential to	(Unit 21)
be exposed to	(Unit 23)
be + constantly [always / all the time 等] ...ing	(Unit 1)
be + to-infinitive	(Unit 13)
be likely to	(Unit 4)
be limited [restricted] to	(Unit 2)
be made of	(Unit 21)
be of the opinion that	(Unit 6)
be related to	(Unit 13)
be similar to	(Unit 5)
be said to	(Unit 4)
be the first to	(Unit 21)
be trapped in	(Unit 24)
be unlikely to	(Unit 24)
be vital for	(Unit 3)
be wiped out	(Unit 4)
become aware of	(Unit 9)
begin to	(Unit 15)
belong to	(Unit 20)
by accident	(Unit 15)
by the end of	(Unit 6)

C

carry out	(Unit 18)
carry ... from ... to	(Unit 23)
close to	(Unit 1)
compared to	(Unit 3)
continue to	(Unit 15)
cut down on	(Unit 11)

D

date back to	(Unit 8)
deal with	(Unit 1)
depend on	(Unit 14)
despite the fact that	(Unit 2)
die from	(Unit 17)
disagree with	(Unit 10)

USEFUL EXPRESSIONS & WRITING

do away with (Unit 22)

E
enable ... to ... (Unit 23)
end up in ,,,ing (Unit 22)
even though (Unit 9)
eventually (Unit 24)

F
fall asleep (Unit 17)
fall victim to (Unit 5)
feed on (Unit 22)
fewer than (Unit 17)
force ... to (Unit 3)
form a boundary between (Unit 6)
free of (Unit 6)

G
get + O + to不定詞 (Unit 5)
get rid of (Unit 2)
get through (Unit 12)
give birth to (Unit 2)
grow up (Unit 7)

H
hold out (Unit 18)

I
if (Unit 24)
in addition to (Unit 4)
in fact (Unit 20)
in other words (Unit 2)
in response to (Unit 11)
in search of (Unit 5)
in the hope(s) of (Unit 8)
in the middle of (Unit 9)
instead of (Unit 20)
it ... for ... to (Unit 7)
it seems that (Unit 2)

it takes ... to (Unit 22)
it is ... that 強調構文 (Unit 7)
it's been suggested that (Unit 10)
it's conceivable that (Unit 19)
it's doubtful that (Unit 18)
it's estimated that (Unit 2)
it's possible to (Unit 19)
it's said to be (Unit 9)

K
keep ... from -- ing (Unit 11)
know of (Unit 20)

L
lay an egg (Unit 12)
lead to (Unit 1)
lead ... to (Unit 14)
let ... 原形 (Unit 24)
look like (Unit 20)

M
make ... possible (Unit 10)
make sense (Unit 2)
meet with (Unit 5)

N
name ... after (Unit 9)
neither A nor B (Unit 5)
no matter what (Unit 19)
not all (Unit 9)
not only that, but (Unit 22)

O
on all fours (Unit 7)
on ...ing (Unit 20)
one ... others (Unit 16)
on the other hand (Unit 8)
once (Unit 1)
once every ... (Unit 15)

P

participial construction 分詞構文	(Unit 7)
play a part in	(Unit 1)
play a role in	(Unit 6)
prey on	(Unit 5)
provide A with B	(Unit 12)
provide clues about	(Unit 3)
put forward	(Unit 8)

R

range from ... to	(Unit 9)
rather than	(Unit 22)
refer to	(Unit 11)
regard ... as	(Unit 11)
rescue ... from	(Unit 7)
result in	(Unit 6)
ride down	(Unit 3)
rumors abound	(Unit 8)
run into	(Unit 8)

S

search for	(Unit 19)
set ... apart from	(Unit 14)
set in	(Unit 12)
set up	(Unit 15)
so ... that	(Unit 20)
some ... others	(Unit 9)
... spell of ...	(Unit 6)
start to	(Unit 10)
stick out of	(Unit 8)
succeed in	(Unit 1)
such as	(Unit 10)
suffer from	(Unit 17)
superlative + that ever + past	(Unit 14)
swarm with	(Unit 8)
switch to	(Unit 22)

T

take from	(Unit 18)
take in	(Unit 7)
take into	(Unit 23)
take place	(Unit 12)
that [those] of	(Unit 10)
the amount of	(Unit 23)
the best way to	(Unit 19)
the chances of	(Unit 18)
the former ... the latter	(Unit 16)
the last time	(Unit 4)
the naked eye	(Unit 21)
the problem is that	(Unit 18)
the reason ... is	(Unit 15)
the twists and turns	(Unit 12)
the way + S + V	(Unit 14)
therefore	(Unit 3)
there is no doubt that	(Unit 1)
think about	(Unit 3)
think of	(Unit 23)
... times	(Unit 4)
to one's surprise	(Unit 3)
too ... to	(Unit 13)
travel through	(Unit 17)
turn into	(Unit 12)

U

unlike	(Unit 23)

V

vice versa	(Unit 13)

W

what interests ... is	(Unit 23)
what they call	(Unit 11)
what would happen if	(Unit 15)
whenever	(Unit 17)
, whereas	(Unit 16)
, while	(Unit 21)
with ... p.p.	(Unit 5)

TEXT PRODUCTION STAFF

edited by	編集
Eiichi Kanno	菅野 英一
Kimio Sato	佐藤 公雄
cover design by	表紙デザイン
Ruben Frosali	ルーベン・フロサリ
text design by	本文デザイン
Ruben Frosali	ルーベン・フロサリ

CD PRODUCTION STAFF

narrated by	吹き込み者
Katie Adler (AmE)	ケイティー・アドラー（アメリカ英語）
Bill Sullivan (AmE)	ビル・サリバン（アメリカ英語）

Science Updates
最新科学の知見

2016年1月20日 初 版 発 行
2024年8月30日 第8刷 発 行

編著者　永田 博人
　　　　Bill Benfield
発行者　佐野 英一郎
発行所　株式会社 成美堂
　　　　〒101-0052　東京都千代田区神田小川町3-22
　　　　TEL 03-3291-2261　FAX 03-3293-5490
　　　　https://www.seibido.co.jp

印刷・製本　三美印刷（株）

ISBN 978-4-7919-4783-6　　　　　　　　　　　　Printed in Japan

・落丁・乱丁本はお取り替えします。
・本書の無断複写は、著作権上の例外を除き著作権侵害となります。